WARNING

Shooting and the handling of firearms involves inhearnt and unavoidible risks. Firearms by their very nature can be very dangerous.

This book is designed to provide the responsible citizen with a starting reference into the world of pistol shooting. If you do not have a substantial background in firearms and firearms handling, seek out a responsible trainer before attempting to utilize or impliment the practices, methods, and techniques described in this book.

Always ensure that the condition, loaded or unloaded, of any firearm is known and verified and then verified a second time!

Always use proper safety equipment to include the proper eye protection and hearing protection.

Always refer to the applicable owner's manual provided by the manufacturer for specific instructions.

If you are not capable or not willing to take responsibility for your own actions, do not handle a firearm.

This book is not intended to be a complete or comprehensive guide to firearm operation. This book must be used in conjuction with manufacturers publications.

DISCLAIMER: No one associated with this book, including the author, is or will be responsible for death, injury, loss or damage to property due to the use or misuse of firearms.

NOTE TO READER:

I am not a professional author. I am a firearms instructor by trade and have been for years. I am writing this book using my thought process and mind mapping. I have tried to follow a path that I use when teaching.

This was not written to be a strictly firearms book, but I have placed a very heavy emphasis on the modern semi auto pistol and the techniques that I think work best.

This book also contains a bit of my own psychology in an effort to put the reader in the correct mindset to be a responsible citizen.

I strongly urge you to seek out qualified instructors for your martial arts training and weapons training.

This particular book touches on basics to advanced principles and techniques. More detailed instructional books on individual concepts will be available soon.

Modern American Combative Arts

KYLE A. BARRINGTON

Volume I – A Guide to Self Defense with a Pistol

Responsible Citizens Seeking Responsible Training

Kyle A. Barrington

Your gun and good intentions mean absolutely nothing without proper training. You are responsible for every round you shoot!

Kyle at the shooting range with wife, Cindy. She is a 4th Degree Black belt (Master) in Tang Soo Do and the owner of Family Martial Arts in Woodbine, Georgia.

A gun is a tool, no better or no worse than any other tool: an axe, a shovel or anything. A gun is as good or as bad as the man using it. Remember that.

A responsible Citizen supports the 2nd Amendment and should seek out Responsible Trainers and quality instruction!

I teach the professionals, but my passion is teaching the responsible citizen.

I will take you as far as you care to go! A responsible citizen must realize that a gun and good intentions mean nothing!

Responsible Citizens Seeking Responsible Training

Each responsible gun owner that seeks out professional training is a responsible citizen!

I am a professional, I have trained people from various backgrounds.

I choose to train the responsible citizen that realizes that their good intentions alone are not sufficient to protect their loved ones!

Let me help you to become the responsible citizen with the training needed to safely and effectively protect all that you cherish!

SELF INTRODUCTION

Kyle Barrington is the owner of Modern American Combative Arts and is a Retired United States Army Special Forces Combat Veteran and Senior NCO.

As a Green Beret I performed the duties of Assaulter, Master Breacher and Special Forces Advanced Urban Combat Instructor. I have earned a Bachelor of Arts in Leadership and Master of Science in Security Management.

I am a Firearms Instructor. As a Lead Instructor for the Federal Law Enforcement Training Center, I was responsible for the Reactive Shooting Instructor Training Program (RSITP). I was instrumental in the development of the Advanced Pistol Training Program (APTP) and the Advanced Pistol Instructor Training Program (APITP). As the Lead Instructor over these programs, I ensure that the knowledge is passed on.

I have spent years as a Federal Firearms instructor ensuring that federal, state, and local law enforcement officers could safely perform basic and advanced firearms techniques.

I am an Adjunct Firearms Instructor for the Sig Sauer Academy and a National Rifle Association Certified Instructor and a Training Counselor.

I have studied various Martial Arts and hold 1st Dan Black Belts in Yoshin Ryu and Goshin Jujitsu and a 3rd Dan in Bujitsu.

I have worked as a combatives Instructor for various US Army Airborne and Special Forces Units while on active duty and after retiring.

Since I retired from the U.S. Army Special Forces and started working for the Federal Law Enforcement Training Center, I have used my shooting and combatives knowledge to start my own business, Modern American Combative Arts. I enjoy teaching "those guys," the professional in the field that carries a gun on a daily basis; however, it is the basic citizen that is looking to broaden the knowledge for every day carry to protect their families that I see the most room for the spreading of knowledge. Teaching firearms and their safe use is my passion!

In the process of writing this book many events have occurred. The news media continues to assault the second amendment. The masses clamor for police protection and for punishing the many for the actions of the few.

I need every responsible gun owner that bought their gun to protect themselves and those that they love to understand that in the United States, a police officer does not have a legal duty to protect the general public.

There are multiple court cases that uphold that it is a *fundamental principle of American law that a government and its agents are under no general duty to provide public services, such as police protection, to any individual citizen.*

I train law enforcement officers and federal agents every day, and I believe that given the time, they will, because of their moral make up, try to "protect and serve." Every statistic that I have found says that the since the police will show up after the incident has concluded, the main job of the any law enforcement agency is to solve a crime after it has happened, not to prevent it.

It is your right to own a firearm and to protect yourself and those you love. If you choose to rely solely on the police to protect you, then you choose to be a victim.

If our law enforcement agencies were obligated to protect us, most often there would not reach the scene in time enough for them to do it. Never abdicate the responsibility for your own personal safety, and that of your loved ones, to anyone else. Seek responsible training.

Always remember the riots in Los Angeles and New York when the police were out manned and had to protect themselves and not the citizenry; remember every shooting that takes place in a soft target like a school; people are injured or killed often before the police can respond. If you make the conscious decision to not be a victim, then you must also make the conscious decision to protect yourself and loved ones in a responsible manner. Seek out a responsible trainer; seek out knowledgeable individuals that will provide you with options for consideration.

Purchase the very best gun you can afford. A gun is nothing more than a tool that should become an extension of you. Not all tools are created equal. Train as much as you can. Train safely and responsibly.

PRINCIPLES NOT TECHNIQUES

SURPRISE, SPEED, VIOLENCE OF ACTION

A well-regulated militia, being necessary to the security of a free state, the right of the people to keep and bear arms, shall not be infringed.

Responsible Citizens Seeking Responsible Training

Protect your rights, protect yourself, educate yourself, and safely learn the modern martial art.

http://www.modernamericancombativearts.com/

www.**modernamericancombativearts**.com/youtube.htm

www.facebook.com/modcombat/?nr

https://www.instagram.com/**modernamericancombativearts**

ACKNOWLEDGEMENTS:

I had several teammates over the years that exposed me to various forms of Marital Arts and Fighting systems, David Sgro taught me F.IG.H.T. AND C.U.T. Combatives (Fully Integrated Grappling & Hitting Techniques, Close-Up Techniques) in Fayetteville, North Carolina. I became an instructor for Dave while also continuing my Japanese and Brazilian Ju jitsu. The L.I.N.E.S. System taught by Ron Donvito in Fayetteville, North Carolina was also a system we were taught. I had the privilege of rolling with several great Brazilian Ju Jitsu students and with Greg Thompson from Raleigh, North Carolina. Greg was running Team Rock at the time and as the Tactical Operations NCO for the 3rd Special Forces Group Commanders Inextremis Force (CIF). I contracted Greg to teach Hand to Hand Combatives and Ju Jitsu to our Special Forces warriors. Because of Greg, I was given the opportunity to be triangle chocked-out by Royce Gracie on two separate occasions. Jon Conell was a true martial artist, teammate and one of the baddest men I have known. Brain Mayfield a friend who exposed me to Hop Gar Kung Fu and presented a model that I still use to teach and explain the "math" of combat. I have been exposed to and trained with many Martial Arts Masters, Sensei's and Soke's while training at the Academy of Christian Martial Arts in Fayetteville, North Carolina, to include Michael Fraley the current owner of Academy of Christian Martial Arts and Special Forces bother who allows me to vent when needed.

The United States Army and the Special Forces taught me how to employ multiple weapons systems. Many good

Responsible Citizens Seeking Responsible Training

team mates and Green Beret instructors helped to form my opinions on firearms. The cadre of Range 37 at Fort Bragg, North Carolina (particularly my good friend "Super" Dave Harrington) who were my instructors for Special Operations Techniques and Special Forces Advanced Reconnaissance, Target Analysis, and Exploitation Techniques Courses. My teammates from the 3rd Special Forces Advanced Urban Combat Instructor Team and my team sergeants, Michael Stack and later Steve Park who allowed me to push the limits in SFAUC.

Steve Park and I continued with Northrop Grumman applying the skills, teaching the principles and techniques to the nuclear security cops for the United States Air Force.

To my fellow instructors at the Federal Law Enforcement Training Center, Ross Begnaud and Mark Missildine that helped me preach the principles that will help protect those that protect our homeland. Jim Palmer, my Branch Chief, and Scott Donavon, my Division Chief in the Fire Arms Division, that allowed me the freedom to take the Reactive Shooter Instructor Training Program and update it, push the limits while creating the Advanced Pistol Instructor Training Program. This allowed me introduce the evolution in the concepts of a Sighting Package, a Movement Package and an Environmental Package and this is becoming a forward way of thinking, training and instructing the martial art of shooting.

The men of the Sig Sauer Academy that continue to amaze me and keep me on my toes, helping me refine my techniques and neurological imprinting. Adam Painchaud who provided me a platform to grow and challenge myself. Scott Reidy and Steve Gilcreast who provided knowledge from the commercial side of shooting and pushed me to use it. Scott Kenneson, who continues to mentor and provide vast amounts of information without always realizing the pearls of wisdom and nuggets of knowledge he provides to me. John Hollister who has opened up the world of suppression and silence. Hana Bilodeau who continually reminds me to have fun teaching.

Sheriff Jeff Brown for deputizing me and allowing for another conduit to pass along the knowledge of responsible shooting.

There are many others that I have run across, trained and fought with over the years and travels. I want to thank you all for helping to shape my views and make me realize that principles, not techniques win confrontations.

I included all my forms of martial arts and fighting system, to better explain my mindset and fighting beliefs.

My Daughter Candas Barrington for all the technical support and for putting up with my anti-machine and computer rants!

James Barrington
I do want to thank my son for helping me finish this book and being my demonstrator.
James has attended US Army Basic Training and is a graduate of the US Army Infantry School. He is an 11B and currently serving as a 12B in the Georgia National Guard.
He is currently attending college and working as a role player at the Federal Law Enforcement Training Center.

Thank you to Ben Turrell of Ben Turrell Photography in Woodbine, GA. for taking the majority of the pictures, well, all of the good ones!

Shot Show 2016 Las Vegas. Working the Sig P320 Booth

*Right to Left: Rich Morvitz-Sig Corporate trainer,
Kyle "Panda" Barrington-Instructor
Kyle Lamb- Viking Tactical,
Kerry Davis- Dark Angel Medical*

Responsible Citizens Seeking Responsible Training

An Excellent exchange of information with the legendary Ken Hackathorn and Daryl Holland

I was privileged to provide assistance from the Sig Academy to a project that Ken Hackathorn and Daryl Holland where working for an allied government.

Ken Hackathorn is a legend in my world and it was a true instructor reaffirming experience for me.

Spending time and bouncing around instructor knowledge with my good friend "Super" Dave Harrington.

Anytime our paths cross I enjoy the "skull sessions" with Super Dave. A true one of a kind and knowledgeable instructor.

Responsible Citizens Seeking Responsible Training

The Final Acknowledgement:

Mostly, I have to thank my wife Cindy for being my better half and putting up with all my ranting, raving and BS over the years!

TABLE OF CONTENTS

Philosophy
Safety Rules
MINDSET   **34**
The Formula
The Mission
Dominate the Adversary
Eliminate the Threat
Control the Situation and the Personnel
My Goal
The Human Response
Practice Visualization
Stress Inoculation through Realistic Training
Types of Fighting: Fighting Distances
Antisocial and Asocial Violence
Basics of Violence
The Human Body as a Target
The Methodologies of Responsible Shooting
Martial Arts Stance
Get Up in Base
UNDERSTANDING YOUR TOOLS   **94**
Pistol
Types of Pistols
Types of Ammo
Holsters
BUILDING SHOOTING FOUNDATION   **121**
Clearing the Pistol
Types of Shooting Stances and Platforms
Dry Fire
The Grip
Biometric Indexing
Presentation from the Holster
Working Area
Broomstick Drill
LOADING/UNLOADING/MALFUNCTIONS 179

Responsible Citizens Seeking Responsible Training

Loading
Press Checks
Unloading
Reloads
Tactical Reloads
Primary Malfunctions
Secondary Malfunctions
SEEING WHAT YOU'RE SHOOTING 205
Sighting Package
Sight Alignment
Sight Picture
Acceptable Sight Picture
Float the Dot
Soft Focus
TRIGGER MANIPULATING 216
Trigger Control
Follow Through
Recovery
Multiple Shots
Flash Sight Picture
Natural Point of Aim
MOVING WITH YOUR PISTOL 227
One Step Movements
90 Degree Pivots
180 degree Pivots
ENVIRONMNETAL PACKAGE 250
Environmental Package
Barricades
One handed Techniques
Close Quarters
Seated
Kneeling
Low Light Fundamentals
ADDITIONAL INFORMATION 284
Team Room Wall / Favorite Shooting Drills

PHILOSOPHY

At Modern American Combative Arts, I believe that fundamentals are the cornerstone of survival and everything is built on basics. There are no advanced techniques. The so-called 'advanced' shooter merely executes the basics to perfection on demand. An advanced shooter practices not until they get it right, they practice until they cannot get it wrong.

Any shooter who wants to improve their shooting, does so only by understanding the basics at a deeper level and practicing the basics until the action becomes ingrained to your neurological pathways.

The 'Combat Triad' consisting of Marksmanship, Gun-handling, and Mindset must be imprinted into your neurological pathways. This will allow your mind and body's kinesthetic ability to take over. This will allow for multiple actions to take place while solving tactical problems.

Ironically, it is usually only the truly 'advanced' student who fully appreciates the importance of continuously refocusing on the basics. A basic shooter **practices until they get it right**; a truly advanced shooter practices until they can't get it wrong.

In this book I will attempt to document and explain what I have learned over the many years of shooting and instructing. My martial arts and fighting views have grown and have changed over the years. Even when I have agreed and disagreed with many good firearms instructors, I still

Responsible Citizens Seeking Responsible Training

learned from them. I will present principles and show techniques that support what I believe. It must be understood that the employment of firearms is in fact a martial art and that like any other martial art there are few truly new things, but rather, just new ways to look at them. The example I most often use is that the current love affair with the various forms of Krav Maga: a pistol takeaway is the same as a 2000 year old sword disarm. As new tools emerge, it is often the *old ways* that continue to work. "Aim small, miss small," nothing more than acceptable sight picture!

With any Marital Art, which shooting most certainly is, the pistol is a tool that can perform the role of projecting a defensive posture, or even an offensive posture in the hands of a skilled operator out to extended distances. I do not believe there is any technique that is a *secret,* or any skill craft that is unknown. What I will present is the principles that I have learned, that have worked for me in hostile situations, and that I believe in.

I have trained with some truly amazing martial artists and some truly bad men and teammates. My martial arts journey began in Taiwan as a child. My father was a career Navy man and stationed in Taiwan. The local Navy recreation center had classes in judo. In my youth I earned the green belt rank and received my first exposure to the martial arts world. My deployments as a United States Army Special Forces Operator into harm's way guided me to where I am now in relation to my martial arts.

I have been exposed to many martial arts systems, and because of this I would encourage any practitioner to study as many arts as possible. I have found that as I age my treachery has grown and my flexibility and injuries over the years have helped to change my outlook and ability to use different fighting systems.

As a member of the United States Army Special Forces (the Green Berets) for 16 years, my exposure to various systems grew. I have found that there are many different techniques

that can be employed in various situations that work. Use a technique that supports a principle, and you will increase your chances of being successful. Put as many tools in your tool box as you can. Many techniques can support a given principle, but I have found over the years that age and injuries will help an artist picks the one that will be best employed.

TRAINING PHILOSOPHY

Within the gun and training industry there are many trainers and a great deal of students that want to be high speed and low drag! The desire is to buy and use AR style rifles and expensive decked out battle belts. Training sessions with these can be fun to teach and are enjoyed by the students, but students pay large sums to take the class.

So, I would ask the responsible citizen to look at where you live; what are the most likely and worst-case scenarios that you are likely to encounter? Do you have a job that requires the tactical employment of an AR rifle system? What gun are you planning on carrying every day?

Look at your current skill set. Can you draw your everyday carry (EDC) pistol from concealment and fire your defensive rounds into an acceptable target zone in an acceptable time?

The stats that the industry uses are three rounds in three seconds fired from three yards in low light? So, remember 3-3-3 in low light is the standard!

I have included the Ken Hackathorn Wizard Drill in this book. I love the drill, and I use it in all my classes as a cold shoot demonstration. The drill is designed to be shot at the 3, 5, 7, and 10-yard lines with duty ammo in a very short prescribed time. The drill often humbles the professionals from the field that have carried guns for a living for 10 years or more.

As a responsible gun owner, you must evaluate your current skill set, look at your needs and be able to perform to perfection on demand.

I find that most responsible citizens would be better served with buying more quality ammunition and range time and practice with the pistol that you bought to save yourself and those you love.

Remember that in concept of shooting, a pistol is a very simple thing. Manipulate the trigger from front to rear without disturbing the sights! This is to proper sight alignment and trigger control. In practice this is not as simple as it sounds.

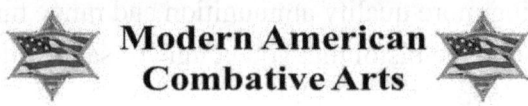

FIREARMS SAFETY RULES

Never point a weapon at anything or anyone UNLESS you have made the conscious decision and are willing to destroy your intended target

Keep your finger off the trigger UNLESS you have made the conscious decision to shoot

1. Treat every firearm as if it were loaded.
2. Always keep the gun pointed in a safe direction.
3. Always keep your finger off the trigger until ready to shoot
4. Be sure of your target/threat, backstop, and beyond.

Shooting a pistol by its very nature is inherently dangerous and all precautions must be made to ensure that the shooter goes home only with the holes that they showed up with.

Many of the techniques that I will discuss will cause the shooter to bring the muzzle of the weapon close to the body. Always treat every weapon as if it is loaded until you, as the weapons handler, are absolutely sure that it is not. Never point the weapon at anything that you have not made the conscious decision to shoot. Know where your finger is and never point the gun at yourself or anyone else while training. **Know what is behind your target, in front of your target and around your target**. This is important on the range and in real life. As a responsible citizen you are responsible for every round you fire.

If you are going to engage in firearms training, invest in approved safety glasses and wear them no matter what type of target you are shooting.

Invest in a good set of "ears". Hearing protection is important. I always wear electronic hearing protection because as an instructor, I like to be able to hear and converse with my students. It may be important to wear double hearing protection. A set of foam insertable ear plugs underneath your outer hard-shell hearing protection.

Humans are born with very few natural fears; loud noise is one of them. The anticipated noise of the firearm going off may cause the shooter to use a flinch response. Double hearing protection will often help manage this.

Always review the firearms safety when you go to the range. Look for and understand additional local range safety rules.

Instructors should always provide a detailed safety briefing! Do not assume all the shooters know the safety rules and understand them.

All responsible citizens should have some type of IFAC (*individual first aid kit*) on them when shooting. I highly recommend any of the kits form Dark Angel or Tactical Medical Solutions. I have known Kerry for years as a fellow adjunct instructor for the Sig Academy. Kerry and Dark Angel provides an excellent Tac Med class. Ross from Tactical Medical Solutions was my team medic on an Afghanistan deployment and he is top notch! As part of your safety planning, I would have to recommend that all responsible citizens have some sort of "gunshot" wound medical training.

I carry the Dark Angel Every Day Carry (EDC) Kit every day at work on the FLETC Ranges!

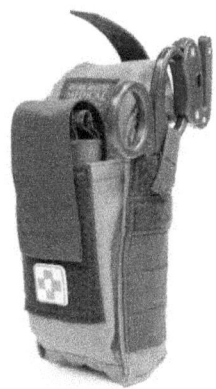

The D.A.R.K. (Direct Action Response Kit) Trauma Kit and Individual First Aid Kit (IFAC) from Dark Angel is the mainstay for all my Tactical Kit setups.

Responsible Citizens Seeking Responsible Training

When preparing for a class and giving the safety briefing ensure that as the instructor you have identified any medically trained personnel in your class and on the range.

If an accident should occur it is important to call 911 and report a *"TRAINING ACCIDENT."* The 911 dispatch does not need to have someone calling and reporting that a person has been shot. We do not want the police responding for an active shooter incident prior to allowing the Emergency Response and Aid Units to arrive.

MINDSET

Responsible Citizens Seeking Responsible Training

When I was training at the Academy of Christian Martial Arts in Fayetteville, NC I met and trained with Brian Mayfield. He introduced me to this formula of combat and I have used it and adopted it over the years.

The Formula= $U/E = (IQ + Aw) \times (A + H) \times (AR + S) = +/- \text{VICTORY}$

You/Enemy= (Intelligence + Awareness) x (Athletic Ability + Health) x (Arena + Scenario)

You/Enemy: Understand who you are, who your enemy is. What is your level of training? What is the training level of your adversary?

Intelligence + Awareness: What is your awareness level? What fighting systems have you learned? What targets are accessible to you? What targets are accessible to your adversary? Did you make the conscious decision to enter this area or where you surprised?

Athletic Ability + Health: What shape are you in? What shape is your adversary in? What is your current health status? What is your cardio shape? What is your mat shape? Are medications or alcohol affecting your health?

Arena + Scenario: Are you in a Dojo? Is this a street fight? Are you in a sporting event? Is it day or night? Is there one opponent or multiple opponents? Are there bystanders? Are you armed? Is your adversary armed?

The principles of combat that I have learned consist of various concepts: Know the Mission, Decisiveness, Surprise, Speed and Violence of Action and keep it simple. This is true in martial sports, arts that are truly martial, fighting and combat in general.

*"**Principles and rules are intended to provide a thinking man with a frame of reference.**"*
Carl von Clausewitz

Responsible Citizens Seeking Responsible Training

The MISSION: The first principle!

You, the responsible citizen must clearly understand what constitutes your mission. Knowing your mission is also a principle. You must decide what your desired end state is going to be. In other words what result are you looking for at the end of a confrontation? Your mind must go to where you want your body to follow. Know yourself!

In <u>The Art of War</u>, Sun Tzu said, *"He who knows when he can fight and when he cannot, will be victorious."*

Your Mission: Prevent harm and the use of violence against you and yours. Fight the fight that affects you and yours! You are only required to fight only the fights that affect you and your loved ones. I will not tell you not to help others or insert yourself into a situation to protect others; I will tell you to check your local laws and to make an informed decision.

In any situation where violence is being threatened upon you or your family, there may come a time when you must make the hard choice, at risk of injury to yourself and those around you, to take the fight to your adversary in a truly violent battle to the death.

Or you can choose to capitulate to your attackers demands, knowing that once you have submitted, allowed yourself to be bound and gagged, the same adversary who invaded your home with violent intent, have nothing restraining them from doing whatever they wish to do to you and your family.

The decision is yours.

Chose to Fight and you MAY get injured or you MAY die.

Surrender and you WILL get injured... emotionally and physically. Whether you live or die will no longer be your decision. You gave up that choice when you submitted. Your fate now rests in the twisted mind of the career criminal standing over you and your family.

The good news, as seen in the home invasions where the occupants chose to fight, is that you have the element of surprise because your attackers are expecting you to submit to their demands.

Actions beats reactions every time, so when you decide to fight, launching a devastating attack quickly and ferociously, with no regard for your adversary's well-being. Look at your adversary as a piece of meat look for your target points, overwhelm them with aggression and don't stop your attack until the adversary is nonfunctional.

If you have a gun and are trained, your attackers will not know what hit them.

Then get a Concealed Weapons Permit and carry your gun with you when away from your home.

If you don't have a gun, get a gun and carry it with you, even in your home.

Know all your options and make the informed decision!

If you make the conscious decision to act, you must act decisively.

Responsible Citizens Seeking Responsible Training

> *"Convince your enemy that he will gain very little by attacking you; this will diminish his enthusiasm."*
>
> *Sun Tzu's <u>Art of War</u>*

Be Decisive. When it is time to act, you must not hesitate!

The second principle!

DOMINATE THE ADVERSARY. A fight is dominated by the responsible citizen moving to points that allow total control of the adversary. The occupation of these points of domination serves to overwhelm your adversary. Domination points are the targets that put your adversary out of the fight, broken bones, ruptured organs, incapacitation or submission.

ELIMINATE THE THREAT. The responsible citizen must effectively eliminate the threat as quickly as possible. This is done through the proper use of force while moving to your points of domination. You must eliminate the ability of your adversary to continue the attack

Look at the hands. A weapon in an individual's hands is the most positive means of identification of a threat. Weapons include firearms, any edged weapons, and anything else that you deem a threat.

Be alert for threatening actions. You must use the proper amount of force for any action that you perceive as a threat. To hesitate may be a fatal mistake. The individual is the only one who can determine whether or not he thinks a particular action or individual is a threat.

CONTROL THE SITUATION AND THE PERSONNEL. It is essential that in the initial few moments of an altercation to maintain control of the situation. Immediately begin speaking to any people in a loud, commanding voice and you must take charge.

EXAMPLE: "Show me your hands"; "You call 9-1-1"

Commands should be short and to the point, and it should be loud enough to be heard by those whose hearing may have been damaged by the sound of gunfire

The final three primary principles of Combat are contained within this definition are surprise, speed, and the proper use of force. (Violence of Action)

The proper application of these three principles during the conduct of a physical engagement allows the responsible citizen to overwhelm and disable their adversary.

The conduct of an engagement without the application of these three principles is doomed to failure.

Surprise: Surprise, above everything else, is the key to successful mission accomplishment. The element of surprise ensures that the responsible citizen has the advantage of preparedness prior to decisive action. The benefit of surprise to the responsible citizen is that the

adversary is disorganized and unprepared to mount a coordinated defense against you.

Speed: Speed in combat will often act as security. It enables the responsible citizen to utilize the first few vital "surprise seconds" to the maximum potential. On the individual level, speed is best described as a "careful hurry." A responsible citizen should not move faster than they can effectively engage targets.

Speed is not defined as how fast the responsible citizen moves, but how fast they eliminate the threat.

If the responsible citizen is moving too quickly and cannot engage the threat, the principle of speed has been violated, and mission failure or friendly casualties will be the result.

Speed, as it applies to fighting styles, means that the momentum of the responsible citizen does not stop until the objective is reached and all threats have been eliminated or controlled.

Violence of Action or Use of Force: Use of Force can be described as a sudden and explosive action that eliminates the threat with the least chance of compromise. When this is coupled with speed, it enables a responsible citizen to maintain the element of surprise, thereby preventing the adversary from delivering any coordinated or planned reaction.

Violence of Action is not limited merely to massive firepower; it also includes mental conditioning or "mind set." The responsible citizen's mind set is one of complete psychological domination and total control of the situation.

This mind set is achieved through long years of practice and hard training. You must know that you have the ability to successfully handle any situation that may arise.

Remember you must utilize speed, surprise, and appropriate use of force. The proper application of these three principles during the altercation allows the combatant to overwhelm their adversary.

These principles when applied correctly with the proper tool and training will not just allow you to survive, but to win and walk away!

Review: Principles of Combat

1. Know Your Mission
2. Be Decisive – Act Decisively
3. Surprise
4. Speed
5. Violence of Action

My goal is to continue the development of a program and thought process that will allow responsible citizens with a means to deal with noncompliant or combative subjects. Remember that a good program should encompass a variety of topics. These include; striking and close quarter defensive tactics, pressure points, takedowns, weapon retention, ground defense, long gun retention, and tactical simulation training. You need to understand your primary means of defense. The use of your concealed carry permit and the use of deadly force may be your preferred means of self-defense, but you must strive to understand as many fighting topics, techniques and systems as possible. Your program should be comprehensive and prepare you for a variety of encounters or altercations. Use the sport to teach body movements and concepts, and then teach violence and its use!

A very important point to remember is that under stress, fine and complex motor skills deteriorate. The loss of fine motor skills can be overcome with training. The ability of the US Military to train Fighter Pilots and Free Fall Parachutists proves this. It's possible to push the envelope of complex motor-skill performance under stress. This generally occurs with specific, well-rehearsed skills. For example, studies done on top Formula One drivers found that their heart rates averaged 175 bpm for hours on end. These drivers perform a limited set of finely tuned skills with extraordinary speed, under a good deal of stress. As defined by Dave Grossman in his book, <u>*On Combat*</u>, stress inoculation is a process by which prior success under stressful conditions acclimates you to similar situations and promotes future success. Since you're ingraining a

pattern with each repetition, it's crucial that any sort of technique be drilled flawlessly. Even in a controlled environment, with a punching bag for an opponent, poor technique in training will be reproduced when it matters. You can't train sloppy and then expect to perform well. When the trained motor pattern is relegated to subconscious thought, there can be no question that it will be carried out correctly. Complex motor control is going to diminish as your heart rate increases; the exact heart rate at which this happens will depend on your level of fitness and the degree to which you're inoculated against stress. Practice under stress so that neurological imprinting can be achieved.

> *"WE DON'T RISE TO THE LEVEL OF OUR EXPECTATIONS, WE FALL TO THE LEVEL OF OUR TRAINING."*
> *Archilochus*

The concepts and principles discussed in this book are mostly gross motor skills in nature. The more you train and practice under stressful conditions the more motor skills you will retain. Become dedicated to studying your art will ensure that the fine motor skills work under stress.

I have learned that over the years of training that many instructors believe fine motor skills should not be used in training because these skills will be lost under stress. I disagree! When teaching firearms it is important to have the shooter manipulate the trigger from front to rear without disturbing the sights. Trigger manipulation is a fine motor skill! If you can manipulate the trigger under stress, then you can operate a slide catch with the proper training.

I will agree that fine and complex motor skills deteriorate under stress, but by training under stress the deterioration can be minimized. I am not telling you that you have to train in the use of fine and complex motor skills, just realize that their effective use requires more practice.

The human response: Fight, Flight, Posture or Capitulate.

Most martial artists are aware of the fight or flight responses that most people display. These are the most common, but not the only responses. The human response will be determined by fear. This is one of the most basic of human responses. These are survival instincts.

Remember the body cannot go where the mind has not already been. Take time to think about violent encounters. In my rape prevention classes, I often tell my students to think about the darkest most vulnerable terrifying place they can go or be forcibly taken.

The mind has now been there, this will help with the **OODA loop. (Observe, Orient, Decide, and Act).** When you are confronted with a violent situation you should already have a plan, a thought process, and training to help you win. Do not wait until it happens to you to think about it, then it is too late!

Fight: You/Enemy assess the challenge and make the conscious decision to engage your adversary in physical combat or if challenged from a defensive posture, you decide to fight back. If this option is chosen, BE

VIOLENT!!! Generally, the person that is the most violent and doing the most violence prevails.

> *"Courage, above all things, is the first quality of a warrior."* Carl von Clausewitz

Flight: You/Enemy assess the challenge and make the conscious decision to evade the threat by retreating or fleeing. This may be part of situational awareness, go around, cross the street and avoid the potential conflict. Do not fight a fight that you cannot win.

Posture: You/Enemy assess the challenge and make the conscious decision to posture aggressively in an effort to influence your adversary to not fight or to flee. The ultimate goal is to "peacock" and to posture your way out of a fight. The goal is not to fight, but convince your adversary that you are prepared too. This may force your adversary to flee or possibly attack.

Capitulate: You/Enemy assess the challenge and make the conscious decision to submit, freeze, lie down, and ask for mercy. Capitulation is an effort to appease the adversary in hopes of little or no damage being done. Fear has taken over.

> *"The conqueror is always a lover of peace; he would prefer to take over our country unopposed."* - Carl von Clausewitz

The Mind!

Positive mental imagery is a tool that those who are at the top of their game use to maintain and improve proficiency, even when they don't have the resources to actually practice the skills. Fifteen minutes a day of dry practice (under safe and controlled conditions) will make an immense difference in the ability to deliver highly accurate fire during a life-threatening encounter. Fifteen minutes a week would easily make the difference in terms of weapon presentation, sight alignment, and trigger control. But it is up to the responsible citizen to do the training (self-motivation).

Aggressive mindset is an offensive mindset. This leads us to a warrior mindset. Once the need arises that requires the techniques discussed in this book it is too late to learn, if a responsible citizen has never trained to be aggressively offensive, how will they hit the switch and become aggressively offensive?

Are you preparing to survive a gunfight or win a gunfight? The responsible citizen needs to have the mental preparation and mindset to be a winner. The Warrior Mindset is being ready for every situation that you may be forced into, against your will. We do not want to react slowly, the difference between slow reaction and an aggressive reaction is this: slow reaction and you will find yourself in a gunfight, quick pro-active handling of the situation and you will find yourself involved in a shooting.

> *"I think anything is possible if you have the mindset and the will and desire to do it and put the time in." Roger Clemens*

Practice visualization, emerging research shows that warriors who visualize hypothetical high-stress scenarios perform better in actual high-stress situations than those who don't.

For example, those who take part in visual exercises demonstrate better marksmanship than those who skip this technique. There's also evidence that visualizing successful management of high-stress situations reduces a combatant's anxiety and stress response when the events actually occur, thus allowing the fighter to stay in optimal Condition Red or an elevated alert state longer.

Make the visualization as vivid as possible. Incorporate all your senses and emotions. Visualize problems and sticking points, the critical part is always visualize yourself successfully overcoming the problem or obstacle. Never visualize failure. Never rely on visualization alone.

It's important to combine it with tactical practice and role playing. Use task-relevant instructional self-talk. To counter the detrimental performance effects of stress, talk yourself through complex actions as if you were an instructor. Another example of task-relevant instructional self-talk would be to yell out "Tap, Rack, and Reassess!" whenever you encounter a gun malfunction. Don't worry if people think you're crazy. Research has shown that this sort of self-talk can increase performance on both cognitive and physical tasks. The key with this type of self-talk is to keep it brief and positive.

Stress Inoculation through Realistic Training; remember the old saying passed down amongst warriors: *"We do not rise to the level of our expectations. We fall to the level of our training"*. Archilochus‘

In combat, you sink to the level of training and practice. Shooting is a very perishable skill. The best way to overcome the detrimental effects of stress on performance is to inoculate yourself from it altogether through consistent, realistic training. From a self-defense standpoint, this means you need to do more than just go to the gun range to practice your marksmanship or punch the heavy bag in your garage. You'll actually need to train your techniques under the same sort of pressure you'd experience in a real-life situation.

For handgun training, this could be achieved with Simmunitions, UTM or airsoft guns; with hand-to-hand self-defense, live sparring can give you similar stress levels as a real-life fight. With proper, consistent, and realistic training, you can hone your body to perform at optimal levels, even when the going gets the toughest. In the shooting world competition, pro-timers and known time drills can provide the self-induced stress that will help to hone your skills.

Tactical style shooting requires the shooter to be more dynamic and aggressive, taking into consideration all the fundamentals of shooting in a high stress environment. As an instructor you must recognize all eight fundamentals of Tactical Marksmanship; which are Stance (Platform), grip, sight alignment, sight picture, breathe control, trigger control, follow thru and recovery. Instructors should observe and understand all eight fundamentals, even though not all are always explained to the student.

Types of Fighting: Weapons, Striking, Grappling

Fighting Distances

I believe that there are six major fighting distances that a trained individual must be prepared for. Working from the farthest distance to the closest, the distances are: Weapons Range, Kicking Range, Trapping Range, Punching Range, Knees and Elbow Range, Grappling Range.

Weapons Range: We must take into account the modern battlefield, whether in the far-off fields of combat, the local streets of your hometown or even your house. Weapons range can pertain to any shoulder fired weapons system, pistol, bow and arrow or Bo staff. When dealing with an adversary at weapons range, seek cover. Fight from a covered position or use flight from covered position to covered position until out of effective range.

For my purposes, I will discuss the pistol. Check your local laws for concealed carry information for your own protection. I am a proponent of concealed carry, and there are many good and competent concealed carry instructors. If you chose to carry a gun, be trained on it; be proficient and train with it. The bad guys will not have a concealed carry permit, so be prepared for an armed encounter. Also remember that even trained law enforcement officers miss their target about 85% of the time, and that the majority of gun fights take place at less than 10 feet. Do not confuse this with the fictitious "21 foot rule".

The Japanese *Bujutsu* refers specifically to the practical application of martial tactics and techniques in actual combat. Hojitsu is the adaptation to the firearm in feudal Japan. It is my opinion that the martial art instructor that does not account for modern weapons is preparing his students for defeat.

The concept of weapons range is the ability to strike from the greatest distance possible. The Samurai of feudal Japan are known for their hand to hand fighting skills. We must look at history and realize that these skills are deadly and violent because everything up to this point failed! The principle is to strike from the greatest distance possible.

The trained responsible citizen must understand the various distances that a fight can be fought from. Study the various martial arts and also understand that a weapon can be used or employed from all of them.

Kicking Range: Many martial arts forms concentrate on kicks and kicking, these include various forms of karate, Tae Kwon Do and Tang Soo Do among others. Kicking range works well in the Martial Arts Studio. Many martial arts techniques work well for what they were designed for. Many of these techniques work well for unseating a warrior on horseback. These techniques also are much easier to perform when wearing the traditional martial arts uniform. These techniques are still very effective and dangerous when performed by those that are trained in them and practice them. The kicking range can be a few feet, out to several yards depending on the skill of the practitioner.

Trapping Range: Many martial arts forms concentrate on trapping techniques; these include Aikido, Kung Fu and various styles of Jujutsu among others. Trapping range is

generally considered closer than the kicking range, but not near enough to make fist to body contact. Trapping range lends itself to blocks, wristlocks and pushing or flowing movement control. Trapping range is often used in many weapon take-away techniques.

Punching Range: Many fighting forms concentrate on punching techniques; these include boxing, kung fu and various forms of karate. Punching range is when opponents are in close proximity, when a fist can make contact with the opponent's body.

Knees and Elbow Range: Muay Thai and kickboxing are known for the use of knees and elbows. Most other standing martial arts will use various elbow and knee strikes. The knees and elbows are vicious weapons and can provide devastating blows.

Grappling Range: Wrestling and various forms of Japanese Jujutsu, Brazilian Jiu Jitsu, Luta Livre and most other Ground Fighting Style martial arts work in the grappling range. This is the one range that all Martial Arts must account for. In a physical encounter, one of three things will happen. The Grappler will force the fight to the ground, the two combatants will clash and fall to the ground, or the skilled stand up fighter will keep the fight from going to the ground. All martial systems must be prepared to fight on the ground or break and stand up. By learning Ju Jitsu or studying mixed marital arts you can learn to get up in base.

When a fight goes to the ground there a few possible positions that the combatant and his adversary can end up in: the guard, mount, side control. Each of these can be further divided.

The guard is when the combatant is lying on his back with his adversary between his knees. In the sport Jui Jitsu world there are multiple versions of this position. For my purposes I will discuss the closed guard.

In Japanese Ju Jitsu the person with their knees to the outside of the body is in control. This allows the combatant to move his adversary.

When being held in the guard position, the combatant must escape.

The mount is when the combatant is lying on his back with his adversary straddling him. The knees of the top mount person are located to the outside of the hips, so the top mounted person is in control.

The person that is on the bottom must escape.

Variations of the mount include the rear mount, this places the person on the bottom on their stomach and is the worst position you can find yourself in. North/South is also a variation that allows for the person on top to be facing the opposite direction.

A skilled combatant must understand the various distances, the skills employed by those that choose the distance and to be able to articulate why the use of force was justified.

The Three D's

1. **Defense**
2. **Devastate**
3. **Deter**

You should always maintain situational awareness; this will help you maintain a good defensive posture. Do not think that a defensive posture rules out a first strike option. You must take in the totality of the circumstances when making this decision.

When you do strike, it must be a devastating blow. Identify your target, hit hard and make it count.

Maintaining a good defense and launching a devastating attack will deter your adversary. Your adversary may be incapable of continuing the fight for several reasons; the bottom line is that you walk away.

I must encourage training in as many martial systems as practical. After you become accustomed to your martial art, try adding a pistol into the mix. Buy a training rubber red gun and see how your movements must be changed.

When teaching Combatives to soldiers from Fort Bragg, it became important to add the pistol. It becomes import to discover how you can use it and how you can keep your adversary from using it against you. It is important to remember that if you bring a pistol to a fight that you have introduced a weapon that may be used against you.

Practice your art forms in your daily clothing. It is possible to draw your gun in your everyday clothing? Do modifications have to be made? What are the limitations? Practice!

Antisocial and Asocial Violence

Anti-social violence should only hurt your pride. You have a choice to walk away. In a posturing situation you can make the decision to leave or stay. You can talk your way out of this. Anti-social violence is avoidable, survivable and we can use our social skills to solve this type of problem. During a truly asocial act, your adversary *will* act, he *will* attempt to do what he wants and take what he wants, and he *will not* talk about it.

The only way to control this situation is for you to act in a decisive manner. You must be the one delivering the violence, render your adversary nonfunctional. If violence is required, you must act violently. Generally, the person who acts most violently survives.

If you have a choice of whether you will respond with violence, then the problem is social and antisocial behavior can be influenced by social skills. If there is no choice, fight or die, then you have encountered asocial violence.

Asocial violence cannot be handled with social tools. You do not have a choice, you win or you lose. Asocial violence is lethal and not affected by the use of social skills. The most important factor of Asocial violence is that you must act and you must act with decisive action!

Violence is not competition

Most martial arts are conducted in an arena of some type and have rules. A back and forth fight that allows for each combatant to survive. There may be injuries if control breaks down, but the object is never to render your adversary nonfunctional.

When the rules are thrown out," unfair" techniques, low blows and cheap shots are used with the objective to finish the engagement; it is violence and not competition.

Violence is where choice ends. If your ability to choose is taken away you have entered the asocial world. Winning comes in a totally different context.

The responsible citizen should be the person doing the violence. The one doing the violence tends to prevail, while the person that is having the most violence done to them tends to be injured, therefore, saving yourself.

Basics of Violence

There are no rules in violence!

The only weapon you have is your brain. Everything else is a tool.

Do not worry what the other guy is doing; focus on what you need to do.

Act like a predator, destroy your adversary. Maim, cripple or kill. You walk away!

Be the one doing the violence.

Focus on the targets that you need to exploit.

Do not quit.

Do not stop until your adversary is nonfunctional.

Violence is not used to "teach a lesson".

Avoid a situation *if you can*.

The following are fouls in an MMA event and will result in a penalty but are good techniques for an Asocial encounter.

1. Butting with the head
2. Eye gouging of any kind
3. Biting
4. Spitting at an opponent
5. Hair pulling
6. Fish hooking
7. Groin attacks of any kind
8. Putting a finger into any orifice or any cut or laceration of an opponent
9. Small joint manipulation
10. Striking downward using the point of the elbow
11. Striking to the spine or the back of the head
12. Kicking to the kidney with a heel
13. Throat strikes of any kind, including, without limitation, grabbing the trachea
14. Clawing, pinching or twisting the flesh
15. Grabbing the clavicle
16. Kicking the head of a grounded opponent
17. Kneeing the head of a grounded opponent
18. Stomping a grounded opponent
19. Holding the fence (proactive use of your environment)

20. Holding the shorts or gloves of an opponent (use of your adversaries clothing)
21. Attacking an opponent on or during the break (fight when your adversary attempts to rest)
22. Throwing opponent out of ring/fighting area (a good toss into the street!)
23. Spiking an opponent to the canvas on his head or neck (hit them on the ground)
24. Interference by the corner (a little help from your friends)
25. Applying any foreign substance to the hair or body to gain an advantage

Proper Mindset! Understand what your adversary is prepared to do to you. Remember the mission, protect you and yours, win; go home!

Opponent Breakdown

To break down an opponent, many Japanese arts teach a flowing technique. This is a Ju Jitsu strategy to work from onset of a fight to its resolution. This strategy consists of blocking, then strikes/kicks, balance breaking and takedown which lead to a finishing blow. It is often possible with the proper target selection to go straight to a disabling blow.

1. Neutralize the Attack
2. Hit to Stun
3. Hit to Damage
4. Hit to Disable
5. Takedown
6. Finish

Tools of the Bu Jitsu trade:

I embrace the gun as a part of Modern American Combative Arts. The modern martial artist must embrace modern and ancient weapons to remain effective.

The goal of the warrior is to create neurological imprinting that will allow for practiced awareness, the ability to focus, commit and act without thought. Harness the adrenaline and fear, grasp situational awareness and act.

Embrace the gun into the martial arts, and then the warrior continues to be effective against modern as well as ancient weapons.

True modern martial arts have no choice but to embrace modern weapons or else the arts become stagnant as an effective way of creating warriors. All martial arts are developed upon their predecessors. For martial arts to continue and to be effective, the gun and other tools must be incorporated.

The brain is your only weapon all other things are merely tools!

Train safely with your tools.

Learn how to use, clear and ensure any gun is in a safe condition. Use red guns or airsoft guns for training events.

Responsible Citizens Seeking Responsible Training

A quick review of Weapon Safety Rules:

1. **Treat every weapon as if it is loaded, know the condition of your weapon!**
2. **Never point a weapon at something or someone you have not made the conscious decision to destroy, injure or kill.**
3. **Know your target and what is behind it, in front of it and around it!**
4. **Muzzle Awareness**

The human body as a target:

The ancient martial arts provide us with the location of hundreds of targets. There are over hundred pressure points; there are bone, organs and tissue that can be damaged. In an effort to keep it simple and use gross motor skills, we will look at the center line of the body.

Picture a line running down the center of the body, from the forehead to the groin. This is our front target area. The eyes, nose, mouth, chin, throat, sternum, belly, pelvis and groin; these areas provide striking targets at several fighting distances. We must always remember that a firearm is a tool that allows a skilled user to exploit the various target areas from a greater distance.

The rear target area runs from the top of the skull and traces the spine down to the groin area.

The body is again divided in half to access the sides. Follow the line of attack down from the top of the skull to the temples, ears, jugular, collar bone, shoulder joint, elbow, wrist, armpit, ribs, knees, ankles and foot.

The brain controls the body and the spine allows for movement. The brain is designed to shut down and protect itself once a violent blow causes it to bounce around the skull. This is a self-preservation method. Boxers wrap their hands for protection and then wear gloves, this is why they can take so many head blows, the blows are cushioned. The MMA fighter has less hand protection and the blows to the head are delivered without much padding, this is why many cage fights end with a knock out.

The spine when damaged will disable the body by shock, paralysis or death. This area provides a large target area for most weapons systems.

"Principle's- Not techniques! Surprise. Speed, Violence of Actions"!

Kyle Barrington

The purpose of my thoughts and training philosophies is designed to address rapid and dynamic encounters at various distances. This pistol training program is designed to instill the techniques that have been practiced by emphasizing the concept of gun fighting principals and using specific techniques, these include the thumbs forward grip, proper body bio-mechanics, committed shot trigger control, and movement (all of which are designed to enhance the responsible citizen's weapon control and ability to engage multiple targets), these will allow a responsible citizen to dominate the weapon and the situation.

The goal is to modify behavior, develop the individual, to become something better than before, so that the individual can performs at their optimum level given a broad spectrum of circumstances. The real goal of tactical shooting is to prepare responsible citizens to perform in "opposition based" situations. The individuals should be capable of performing when experiencing highly stressful situations. Can you, as a responsible citizen perform on demand? Can you perform when opposed? This is all that matters. Either you can or they can't.

A principal-based approach is universal and applies in all relevant combative arenas. A technique-based training approach focuses on specific methods used to neutralize the adversary.

Techniques are an important part of combat preparation, but they may leave the student with a lack of understanding and a limited approach to winning confrontations. If a responsible citizen only has techniques to rely on and his technique fails in combat, he is left with no principals to fall back on, essentially unable to adapt to the unfolding reality.

In contrast, a responsible citizen who possesses a deep understanding of principals is adaptable. Even if his technique fails, he is capable of recovering and moving forward.

Using these principals, and focusing on efficiency and economy of effort, I hope to develop the responsible citizens weapons handling potential and ability to the point

of being a thought or decision keyed response supported by reflexive weapons handling techniques.

Once the responsible citizen has moved into the reflexive application of training, it is then possible to render a cognizant shoot/no shoot decision based upon what the threat is doing instead of a stress-based response.

Traditionally, firearms instruction has primarily focused on precision shooting. The emphasis has been on smooth trigger operation which does not disturb sight alignment and produces the most accurate shot at any distance up to the effective range of the weapon.

While these are sound principals for basic marksmanship and precision shooting, most deadly force encounters happen too quickly and too close for this type of shooting for the unskilled shooter.

The physiological and psychological changes that happen to the human body under survival stress render most of these fundamentals unattainable without proper training.

A good responsible citizen should practice and be proficient at bullseye shooting. There is a reason the 700, 500, and 300 aggregate courses of fire are referred to as "humblers' and contain bullseye strings! *Drills included in the rear of this publication.*

The best operators in the world are trained to use their sights! The ability to rapidly acquire the sights and apply the basic fundamentals of marksmanship is an advanced skill-set that must be continuously practiced.

I do believe that a skilled martial artist can acquire a proper sight picture under stress. Soft sight focus, hard sight focus, front sight. Depending on the practice and skill the shooter will become better at acquiring the sights which we will discuss in a bit.

Statistics gathered from actual deadly force encounters and studies regarding the physiological and psychological effects of survival stress have revealed that these current training methodologies do not prepare for what may actually happen in a deadly force encounter.

By incorporating skills such as threat recognition, movement, and using new training technologies and methodologies that enable the practice and evaluation of these skills, the responsible citizen should become more confident and skilled when reacting to a deadly force encounter.

My purpose and presentation of Martial Arts based Marksmanship concepts is to improve the shooters ability to master the basics of marksmanship and decision making at realistic combat speeds.

These procedures will provide the necessary skills to overcome a life-threatening altercation. We will focus on the mastery of the basics and efficiency of weapons handling, movement and firearms accuracy under varying levels of stress. This skill set otherwise goes untrained in traditional, static firearms training.

If the brain does not process what it sees, it may not be able to make use of it. Distracted attention is one of the biggest pitfall of soft focus shooting. Though some will process at a subconscious level without recalling it, the ability to remain aware of what is being seen as shooting takes place is a higher level of performance. This requires a higher level of training. The conscious mind feeds the unconscious mind.

By training in the techniques and principles of Martial Arts based Marksmanship the responsible citizen can develop movement and weapon control into a reflexive behavior, thus creating a positive neurological pathway!

Once this neurological imprinting of weapon manipulation is achieved, the shooters should be tested in various shoot/no shoot decision making scenarios that open up their ability to make positive, controlled choices under stress.

There must come a time in the training cycle that realistic type targets are used! There are law enforcement agencies that are not permitted to use realistic targets or targets of varying colors. This is done in an effort to influence their decision-making ability.

In the martial arts world, I have always been taught that the body cannot go were the mind has not already been. As troubling as some may find it, you are training to protect yourself and your loved ones.

If you are ever required to test your skill set. It will be against a realistic target, another human being.

I have witnessed over the years that targets do effect decision making. I do remember when Special Forces had to add faces to our targets. This was done after studies proved that it was needed.

I have witnessed that reasonable people will engage a male target quicker than a female target. This is a byproduct of upbringing. When teaching active shooter classes the incorporation of teenage or child realistic targets are extremely harder for law enforcement officers to engage.

By training under a steadily increasing level of stress and performance standards, the shooter's ability to control the adverse physical and mental reactions to stress is increased. Using the concepts of: dominate the weapon, dominate the opponent, dominate the situation and dominate all visual areas, the shooter uses the specific techniques within the tactical shooting training to overcome and dominate all actual and potential threats generally within a close combat range.

Courses of Fire are a series of drills that when properly used should expand the close and extreme close quarter's distances, to incorporate stopping the threat from the 10 and 15 yard line with increased time to compensate for the distance. As distance increases, time for accurate hits increases. The 25 and 50 yard lines will demonstrate this. A skilled practitioner can process the variables and make very accurate hits at 100 yards and farther with a pistol!

This shooting technique emphasizes the High Thumb grip pioneered by the Office of Strategic Services (OSS) in the early 1940s and embraced in the competition shooting world in the late 1970s and early 1980s. It helps develop the shooters weapon handling potential and ability to the

point of being a thought-keyed response supported by kinesthetic weapon handling techniques. The overall program goal is to transform the shooter from one who is in the reactive threat driven mode to a pro-active, controlled response, problem solving mind-set.

What this means is that you will need to be able to visually process what you are seeing as you are shooting. This allows for rapid acquisition of target, adjustments in sight picture and alignment, and visually calling shots — all done at high speed under the duress of a lethal force situation.

In tactical shooting the shooter must train and prepare for gunfight speed (COMBAT) with unknown (rapid) times, varied distances and rapid trigger manipulation. The shooter must use the entire focal continuum, their natural action platform, movement and acceptable accuracy to acquire accurate hits.

Bottom line is using the sights as much as needed to make an accurate shot on an appropriate target. The more accomplished the shooter, the better the sight alignment/sight picture and smaller the acceptable level of accuracy.

Kinesthetic and peripheral awareness of the weapon are integral to tactical shooting at close distances. As the distance is increased, more focus (on the sights) must be attained to ensure accuracy. This is determined by the acceptable level of accuracy for any given shooter.

As an NRA Training Counselor and Instructor, I start classes shooting paper plates. This has been decided by the NRA as the acceptable level of accuracy.

I will start my tactical classes shooting a 3x5 card on top of a 5x8 card. I will run a version of the F.A.S.T. Drill and these size cards become the level of acceptable accuracy. *This drill is covered in the rear of this publication.*

Then there is a point the B-8 Bullseye becomes the acceptable level of accuracy. The B8 shot at 25 yards will expose all the shooter's imperfections with trigger control and sight alignment.

Responsible Citizens Seeking Responsible Training

Next is moving up to bowling pin type targets, the FBI "Q", the US Marshal "Q" or the FLETC ATT-1 Advanced Pistol Instructor Target. This allows the mind to process information faster but keeps the acceptable level of accuracy where I need it to be.

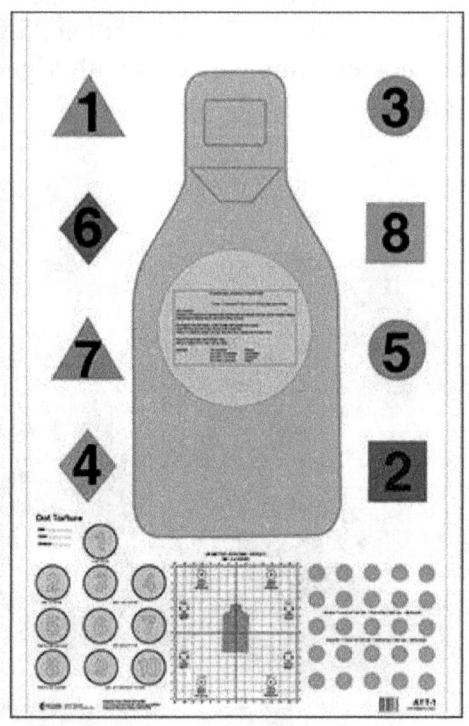

The next progression for my classes is Kyle Lamb's VTAC target. This type of target starts to incorporate the "human" type target. This type of target exposes the internal hit zones.

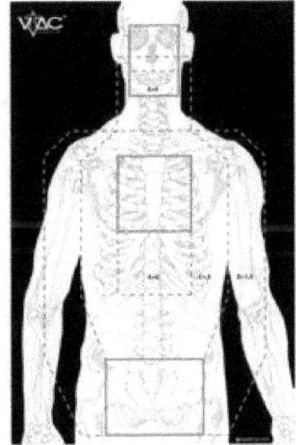

The final type target is the realist type target. This target has a face and is recognized as another human. Only progress to this after your skillset and mindset will allow for it. There may be physiological issues that are encountered. These type targets will force your mind to go to a dark place.

Learn to use your sights and focus on them as hard as you need to place accurate hits on a given type target and any given distance. Do not be afraid to stay up close at the 3 yard line until you have improved your acceptable level of accuracy to where it needs to be.

Then work your way back to the 5, 7, 10 and 15 yard lines. The 25 yard line will expose all your flaws and allow you to move back up and start getting better.

Responsible Citizens Seeking Responsible Training

There will be a time and place that allows for you to shoot a pistol at targets 50 or 100 yards and even farther.

Whatever target you choose, it should be scoreable and force accountability! Do not worry about speed until the ability to consistently place your rounds into your acceptable area of accuracy.

Add some type of pressure as you become more proficient, by introducing the elements of time and peer pressure. Speed will come and is a byproduct of training correctly and demanding accuracy.

Turn your drills and Courses of Fire into competition, maintain accountability for every shot. Learn to call every shot!

THE METHODOLOGIES OF RESPONSIBLE SHOOTING

As shooters, we must understand and be able to discuss the pros and cons of multiple techniques. We must understand that the technique is a way to accomplish the task at hand, not THE way.

Each shooter will have to determine what works best for them. It is also imperative that an instructor understands that just because the *instructor* cannot accomplish the assigned task with the technique chosen; does not mean that the *student* cannot use that technique to accomplish the task.

Do not allow instructor's lack of ability to prevent the student from attempting the technique. The instructor's goal should be to provide the information and then coach the student to use the technique that works best for them. There are usually multiple techniques that will support a skill that does not violate a principle.

Do not confuse competition with combat. Certain competition skills, drills and styles may or may not have a place in the combat/tactical world. An instructor should be familiar with these techniques so that the discussion of pros, cons, whys and why not's may be had.

Responsible Shooters must not forget why we are training and what we are planning to accomplish. We are training to eliminate a threat and this cannot be taken lightly. We are planning to protect our loved ones and to do this we must win, not just survive.

Positive mental imagery is a tool that we need to remember to incorporate to be at the top of our game to maintain and improve proficiency, even when we don't have the resources to actually live-fire practice the skills.

Remember that fifteen minutes a day of dry practice (under safe and controlled conditions) will make an immense difference in the ability to deliver highly accurate fire during a life-threatening encounter.

A responsible citizen should be able to find fifteen minutes a week to ensure the difference in terms of weapon presentation, sight alignment, and trigger control.

Are you truly preparing to survive a gunfight or win a gunfight?

Never visualize failure.

Never rely on visualization alone.

Always remember why you have chosen to carry a firearm and who you are wanting to protect. You owe it to yourself and your loved ones!

Technique Presentation. The average student learns a skill by observing the instructor's demonstration of the technique. In many ways, there is a direct relationship to the student's skill level and the instructor's demonstrations of skills. Therefore, demonstration skills should be carefully articulated and presented, so the student can develop a clear picture to replicate.

A mediocre instructor will tell the student how, a good instructor will explain how, an accomplished instructor will demonstrate and a great instructor will inspire!

Seek out multiple instructors. Go to different classes. Put different tools in your tool box!

Physical Skill Practice. Developing confidence will largely be dependent upon the student seeing an increase in skill level or actually experiencing a successful technique application. In either case; confidence and technique success will be a product of technique fluidity.

The key to successful tactical shooting training is finding methods to decrease the shooter's reaction time to a threat stimulus and provide training which will condition the students to an automatic response without hesitation.

The Martial Arts Stance

A good fighting stance should be comfortable if you are expected to fight from it; you should be able to place yourself into it for extended periods of time. Try to keep your stance simple. A good stance should support all standing fighting styles with very little modifications.

A martial arts stance, a pistol shooting stance and a rifle shooting stance are basically the same. Our eyes are in the front of our head and we are designed to face a threat!

A good fighting stance (platform) will allow you to face your adversary. This stance will support a posture that allows you to diffuse a situation, throw a punch or strike or draw a pistol.

Despite the great number of physical differences in any cross-section of fighters, the stance must provide for the greatest possible degree of equilibrium and stability with the least possible strain on your muscles. To assume the correct stance you must consider the following:

1. Place the feet about shoulder width apart.

Responsible Citizens Seeking Responsible Training

2. Place the support side foot slightly forward of the strong side foot (normally 2 to 4 inches) and point it directly at the target.

3. Distribute your weight evenly over the balls of the feet, providing balance and the ability to move quickly.

4. Bend slightly forward at the waist in order to maintain the center of gravity over the balls of your feet.

5. Stand with your shoulders and head square to your adversary.

6. Raise your strong side arm to eye level and extend it fully, maintaining a slight muscle tension in the elbow and wrist. It is important to keep the strong

side arm as relaxed as possible because excessive muscle tension will be transmitted to the hand and the fingers. Isolate only the muscles necessary to make a fist, ridge hand, grasp a knife or fire the weapon and maintain a minimum arc of movement.

7. Raise your support side arm and hand to join the strong side hand. Extend the support side arm,

maintaining a slight bend in the elbow. Apply slightly more muscle tension to further stabilize any weapon. Be careful not to apply excessive tension, as this will cause excessive strain and an increased arc of movement when shooting.

8. Be aggressive both mentally and physically.

9. Bend forward slightly at the waist to maintain your balance and concentrate on the fundamentals, principles, and techniques.

10. Through practice, this stance will become a conditioned reflex.
11. The fighting Stance IS THE Shooting Platform!

Get pushed down? Get up in Base!

I have already discussed that the possibility of going to the ground in a physical altercation is high. A very basic Ju Jitsu move to return you to your feet is getting up in base. Being able to stand is a critical task. You need to understand what you're fighting stance is. Most people will have their feet slightly wider than their shoulders, knees slightly bent, your back should be straight and you should be slightly tilted forward at the waist.

1. Control your fall (rear falling Technique)

2. Tuck your chin to your chest; this will help keep your head from bouncing off the ground.
3. Never reach back in an attempt to stop your fall.
4. Use your entire arm to act as a shock absorber. Slap out at a 45% angle. Always remember to slap with your palms facing down. This will help dissipate the downward energy.
5. Identify the location of your adversary.

6. Sit up facing your adversary. One hand will be placed behind you, to aid you standing up.
7. The other hand is placed in front of you; between you and your adversary. This hand should be above your bent knee.
8. The other leg can be used for defensive kicking; this will allow you to create space. If you kick the knee is your primary target!

9. To stand up, balance on your down hand and foot. Remember you can strike the knee or inner leg of the adversary if needed to create space.

10. Bend one knee and bring your foot into your body.

11. Bracing on the down foot and hand, coil your kicking leg back in a circular motion. Try to bring this foot back to your down hand. This will create a three-point stance.

12. Remember: Head Up! Know where your adversary is.

13. Stand and draw your forward foot to the rear to help create some space.
14. Our goal is to get from the ground to a two-point fighting stance.
15. Your fighting stance should be the same as your shooting stance.

16. In a violent encounter it may be necessary to fire your weapon from the seated position. (Ensure you dry fire this and follow all weapon safety rules.)

I have continued to stress that shooting is a very advanced and deadly martial art; a solid martial arts fighting-stance is a good place to start your shooting stance. Your shooting stance will allow you to create a much better shooting platform.

Understanding Your Tools

Responsible Citizens Seeking Responsible Training

Pistols

Before discussing and demonstrating the draw stroke and various shooting techniques and positions, it is import to understand the different tools required. These tools must still be used in conjunction with our safety rules. Treat these tools with the same respect that any firearm is given.

Responsible Citizens Seeking Responsible Training

Red Guns are manufactured in many colors, this tool provides a solid pistol shaped training device that is accurate in every detail. I would encourage any student to purchase a red gun that mimics the real pistol they are training with. The proper training weapon will allow for additional weapons training in a safer manner. These tools will need to fit your daily holster and allow for mimicking your real-world training.

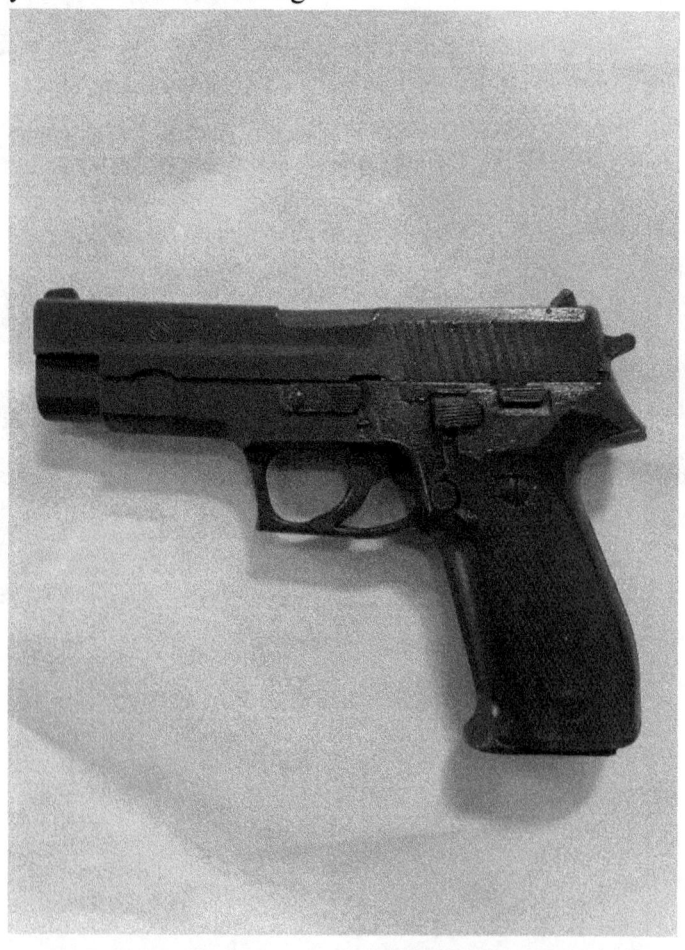

Air Soft training guns also are designed to mimic real weapons. The airsoft gun will have trigger manipulations. Most airsoft guns are exact replicas of your real gun and can be easily mistaken for real guns. Do not rely on the orange ring on the barrel to distinguish the airsoft from the real one.

Responsible Citizens Seeking Responsible Training

Pistol with Dummy Rounds. Always conduct a safety check of any firearm. Once again, back to safety. Know the condition of your weapon and treat all firearms as loaded until absolutely positive that they are not. An UNLOADED pistol will provide actual weight and functions since it is the gun you carry.

Parts of the Sig Pistol

1. Barrel
2. Slide
3. Front sight
4. Rear sight
5. Frame
6. Take-down lever
7. Slide catch lever
8. Trigger
9. Hammer
10. Decocking lever
11. Magazine catch
12. Magazine (seated)

Most pistols will have the same general mechanisms that will perform the same functions. Please refer to the owner's manual provided by the manufacturer that built your pistol and become familiar with it prior to shooting your pistol.

Responsible Citizens Seeking Responsible Training

TYPES OF PISTOLS

Single Action

This is the oldest currently available pistol mechanism, designed by John Moses Browning at the turn of the 19th century. The most famous and noteworthy Single Action variant is employed on the Model 1911 .45 ACP (Automatic Colt Pistol) and the Browning Hi-Power in 9mm Parabellum

In these pistols, an exposed hammer is manually fully cocked and a safety lever mounted on the left side of the frame engaged. To fire, the shooter clicks off (pushes down on) the safety and pulls the trigger, which commonly has a light and short travel, enhancing potential practical accuracy.

With this action type, each trigger pull is short, light and consistent, significantly contributing to ease of use and accuracy. Basically, the hammer is cocked for the initial shot. The trigger pull has one function, to release the hammer so that it travels up to meet the firing pin.

Double Action:

The double action mechanism mimics the trigger and hammer action of the double action revolver. American manufacturers, most notably **Smith and Wesson,** produced double action pistols in large numbers beginning in the 1970s to increase sales of semiautomatics to police forces in an effort to upgrade those that almost exclusively used double action revolvers.

Responsible Citizens Seeking Responsible Training

Double Action Only:

This is a hybrid of the double action mechanism that seeks to address the inherent shot to shot accuracy problem of such actions. These weapons are incapable of single action fire; each pull of the trigger *must* be double action. In other words, the trigger recycles fully forward after each shot–it does not cock the hammer–making a long, relatively heavy trigger pull necessary for each shot. This type of action requires a long, heavy trigger pull that will be inherently less accurate and harder to consistently shoot than a lighter, shorter trigger.

Striker Fired:

The most modern mechanism is the striker-fired pistol, typified by the GLOCK. These weapons do not have an exposed external hammer or an internal hammer, but instead employ what is essentially a larger than usual, heavier firing pin driven by a strong spring.

Glock did not invent the striker fired gun, but they did popularize it. The Sig 320 is now the striker fired pistol adopted by the US Army as the M17 and M18.

When recoil cycles the slide, the striker spring is compressed—cocked–until it is released by the next activation of the trigger. Cycling the slide to chamber the first round does the same. Trigger pulls with this type of weapon are shorter and lighter than those of double action pistols and are consistent from shot to shot.

While the triggers do not have the very short travel of a single action mechanism and they are not as light, they are considered superior to any double action or double action only mechanism, and are also superior to double action revolver triggers.

The striker fired pistol is the easiest type of pistol to teach beginning shooters.

DA/SA

The most common type semi auto pistol is the traditional double single action or DA/SA.

These pistols may be carried with the hammer down on a loaded chamber. Most (but not all) have a passive firing pin block to prevent the firing pin from reaching the primer of the chambered round unless the trigger is pulled fully to the rear. When drawn from this condition, the first long trigger pull cocks the hammer and lets it drop. Subsequent shots are fired from a hammer cocked state, as the recoiling slide cocks the hammer as it cycles to eject the fired casing and strip a fresh round off the magazine to chamber it.

There may be a manual safety on the slide or the frame, or no manual safety at all, as on the SIG. In most cases, engaging the safety lowers the hammer. The pistol may be carried with the safety either engaged or disengaged.

The first shot is fired with a long, heavy double action pull (DA), while consecutive shots are fired with a much lighter and softer single action pull (SA). Considerable training and practice are required to accustom the shooter to this variable mode of operation.

The first shot is especially critical, the longer and heavier double action first pull must be carefully practiced.

The DA/SA is very common and requires a better and more practiced skill set to manipulate. Master the DA/SA and you will become a much better shooter.

Types of Ammo

Dummy

Dummy rounds are totally inert. The bullet is plastic, no primer and no gun powder. The round is designed to allow for the pistol to function. The round is a must for malfunction clearing practice. Everyone should have a handful in their pistol bag.

Ball

Ball Ammunition is designed to mimic defensive or duty rounds. Ball ammunition is a solid bullet and used for training. Ball ammunition will often penetrate much farther than defensive or duty ammunition.

Train with quality ball ammunition that is comparable to your defensive rounds.

Use ball ammunition to train, but do not substitute these rounds for defensive ammunition unless you are living in a jurisdiction that does not allow the use of defensive rounds.

Frangible

Frangible ammunition is designed to mimic defensive ammunition. These bullets are designed to come apart or disintegrate upon impact with steel targets or bullet traps.

Frangible ammunition bullets are often lighter that defensive ammunition and this often requires more gun powder to push the bullet so that it mimics defensive ammunition.

Many of the frangible ammunition manufacturers have gone to "green" nontoxic ammunition. A lot of indoor ranges will require the use of frangible ammunition.

Duty

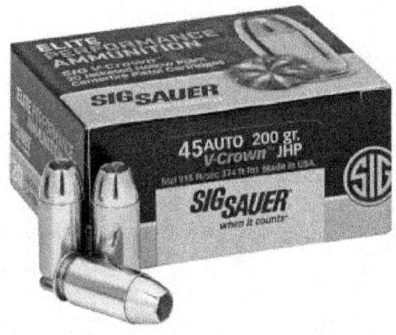

Duty or defensive ammunition is often referred to as "hollow points". These bullets are designed to open up and expand as they impact a semi solid target.

These bullets are needed for personal defense. They are what need to be in your pistol for home defense. These bullets do not over penetrate. *Over penetration is when a projectile does not stay lodged in the intended target. The bullet basically went too far because it was not contained.*

Holsters

As a responsible citizen you have invested a large amount of hard earned money to buy a quality pistol, so invest is a quality holster!

I do not use the holsters that come with the pistol.

Invest in a quality holster that will work in the environment that it will be used.

Ensure the holster that you select covers the trigger and trigger guard.

I own several holsters for each pistol that I use. I like a good Kydex holster. Kydex is a type of hard plastic that is commonly used in the making of a ridged holster or magazine pouch.

Any holster that is worn inside the pants or appendix must not collapse!

A good holster will protect the finish of your pistol and allow for comfortable and safe carry.

A Pocket Holster for a Ruger LCP .380

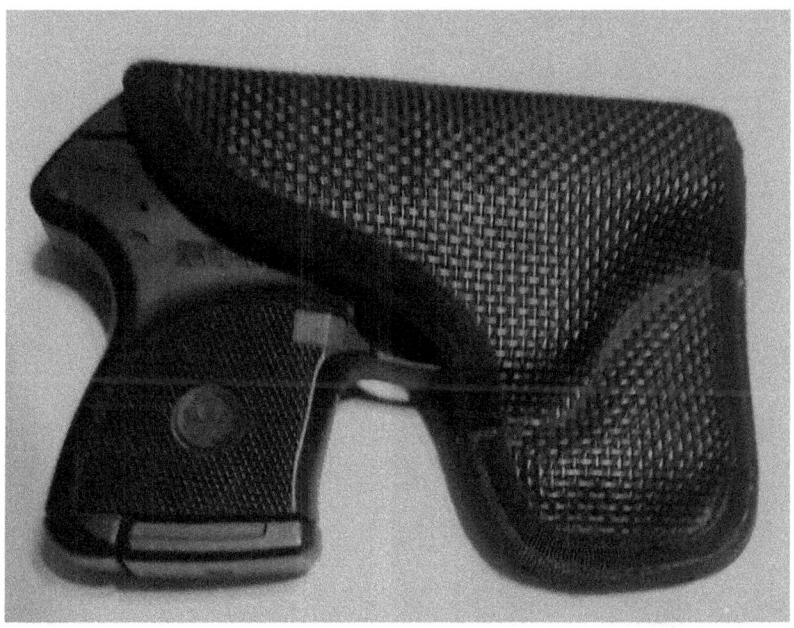

Always put a pocket gun in a holster that covers the trigger!

Responsible Citizens Seeking Responsible Training

Old School Leather Holster

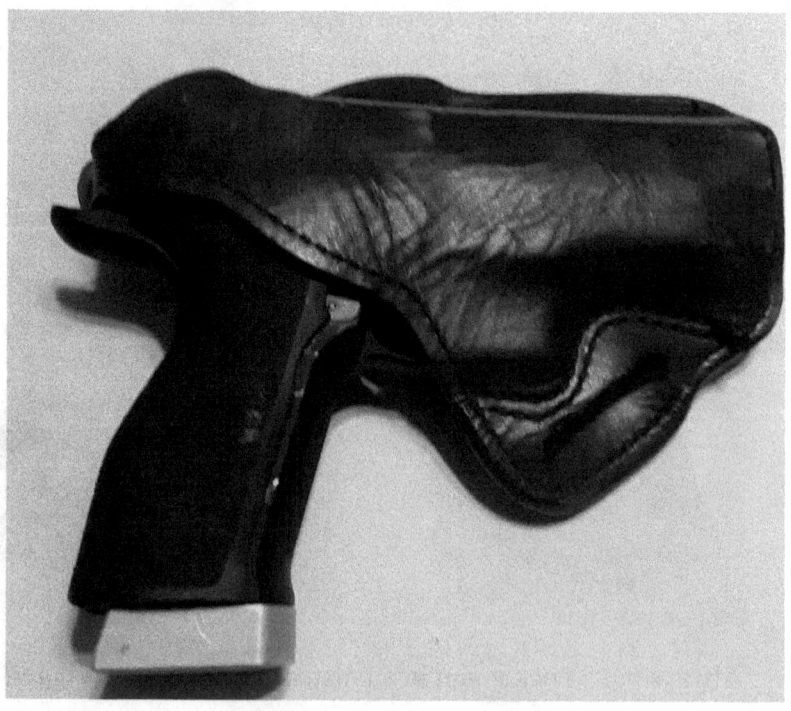

A leather holster requires more care than other holsters, but always comfortable!

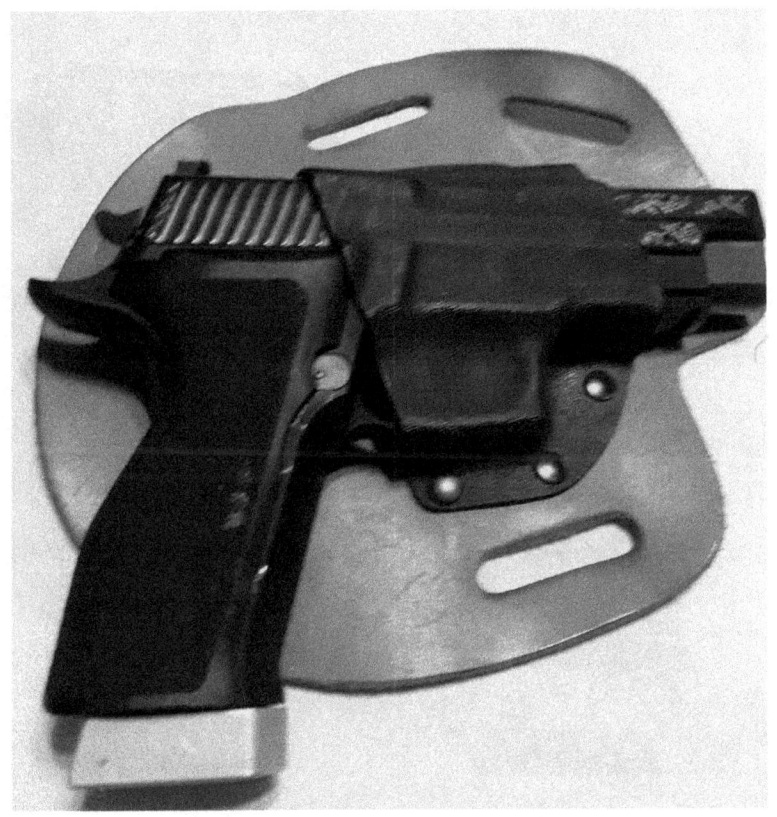

A leather backed with Kydex front

Responsible Citizens Seeking Responsible Training

A beefier version of the leather rear against the body and Kydex holding the pistol

A leather and Kydex inside the waistband holster (IWB)

A Kydex holster with leather wings and one of my favorites

A hard Kydex designed to help incorporate a pistol light

Responsible Citizens Seeking Responsible Training

A full Kydex holster with leather wings, designed for a light/laser combo

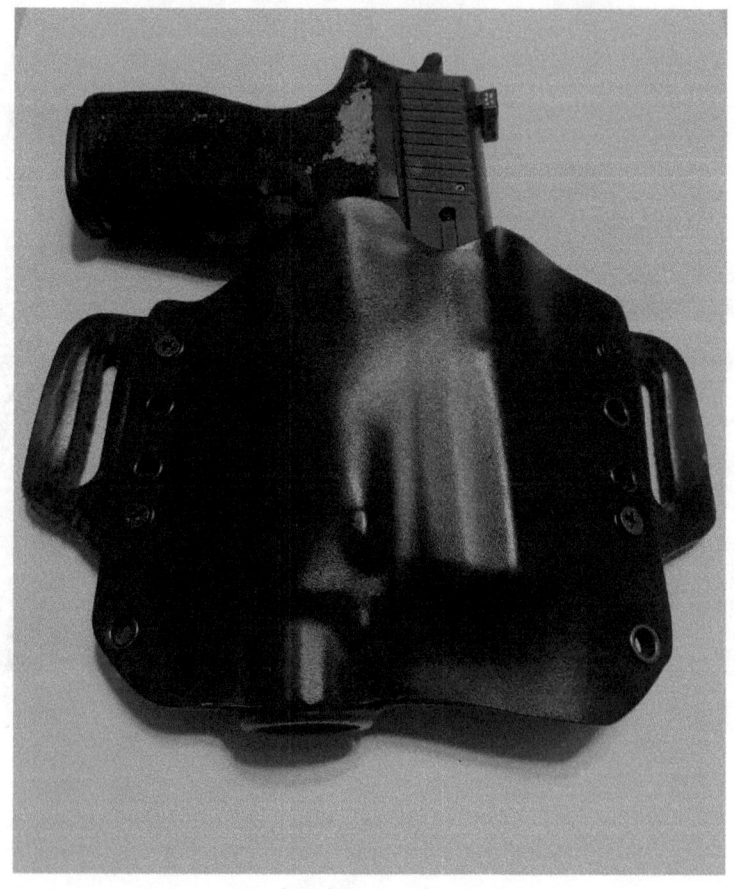

I always advise responsible citizens to buy the best pistol they can afford at the time they buy it. A pistol is a tool, and you do get what you pay for. A holster is a very important part of the equation. I often see people with a $1,000.00 pistol stuck in a $25.00 holster.

Invest in a quality holster that is designed for your gun! I am not a fan of the multi-gun holster. A good holster should be made for your gun. The holster should cover the trigger guard. A good holster should be comfortable for the wearer.

It is advisable to have multiple holsters for one gun. Get a holster that supports your clothing choices. Have an inside the waist band (IWB) and an outside the waist band (OWB) holster.

If you are wearing a holster that is attached to your belt, make sure you have invested in a quality belt!

Building Shooting Foundations

CLEARING THE PISTOL

Instructors and students must understand the semi-automatic pistol.

Safety Rule: Treat every weapon as loaded until absolutely sure that it is not! To accomplish this, we must "clear" the pistol. We want to clear the pistol in such a fashion that it allows for other manipulations as we move forward. Never point the muzzle at yourself or anyone.

With any magazine fed weapon, it is important to first remove the device that feeds the pistol.

Always manipulate the magazine release for the given pistol. Consult the manufactures instruction booklet to locate this device.

The magazine release on most American designed modern pistols is located on the left side of the pistol grip. For left handed shooter this can be switched over to the right side.

Many older pistols will have a European release which is located on the bottom of the magazine well.

Even when you don't actually have the magazine in the pistol, press the magazine release to simulate releasing the magazine, or actually allowing the inserted magazine to fall free. This should be conducted in the same location that the shooter clears malfunctions that will be discussed later.

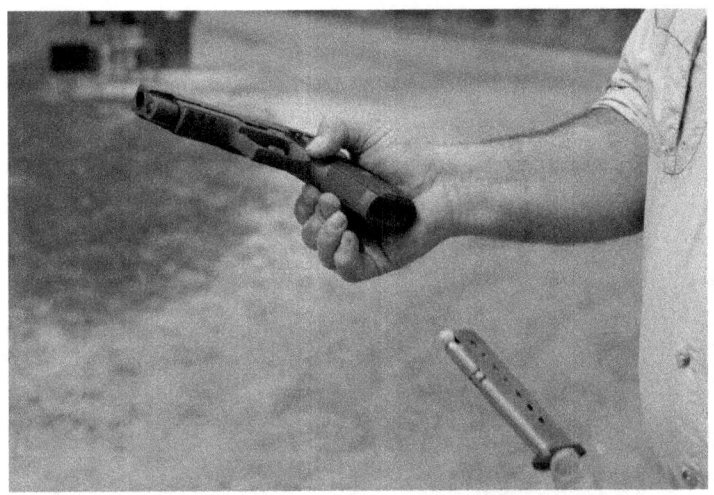

Grab the slide and with a good grip on the pistol grip pull the slide quickly to the rear. Observe to see if and ammunition is expelled. It is recommended that the slide is manipulated multiple times to ensure that nothing is in the chamber of the pistol.

Responsible Citizens Seeking Responsible Training

Lock the slide to the rear. Most pistols will have a slide stop on the left side of the pistol and on top of the pistol grip.

The slide being locked to the rear will allow for a visual and physical inspection of the pistol. There are three potential places that may house a round.

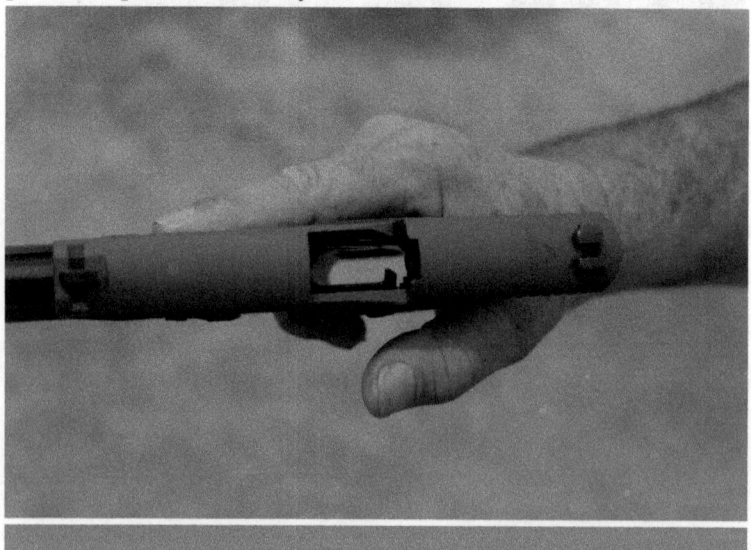

Look directly down the magazine well. If you released the magazine then you should be able to see the floor. When looking for the floor the shooter would notice if a round is stuck on the breach face. If there is a round here, you will not be able to see the magazine well.

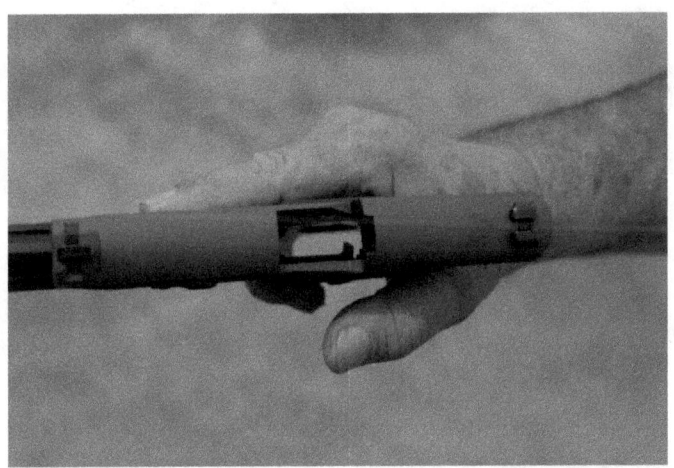

Check the chamber. It is possible that a round is lodged inside the chamber. It there is anything here the shooter will see the rear of the bullet casing.

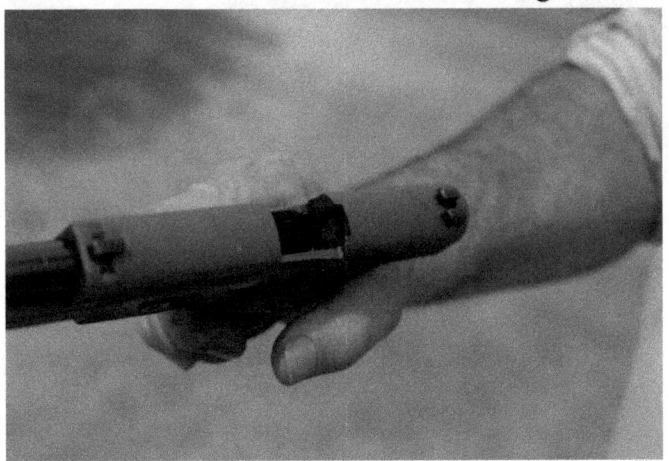

Responsible Citizens Seeking Responsible Training

I recommend checking with your pinky finger to ensure there is nothing there. Look for something, if it is there it will be seen.

Look away and conduct the clearing procedure again!

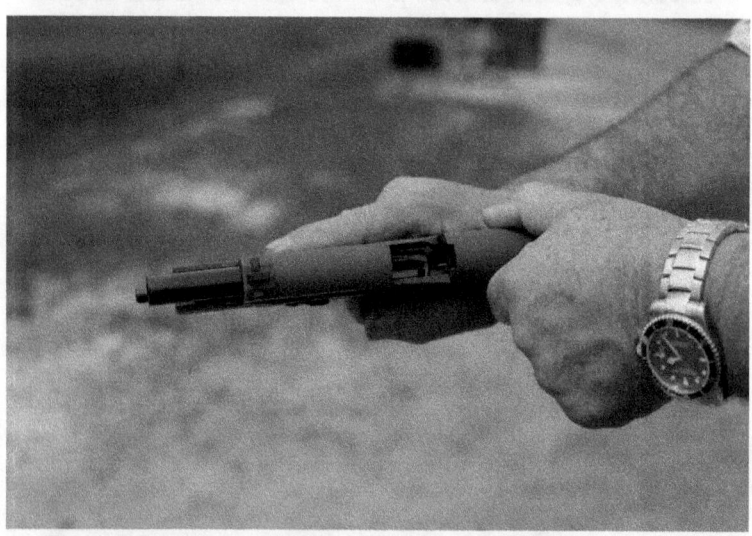

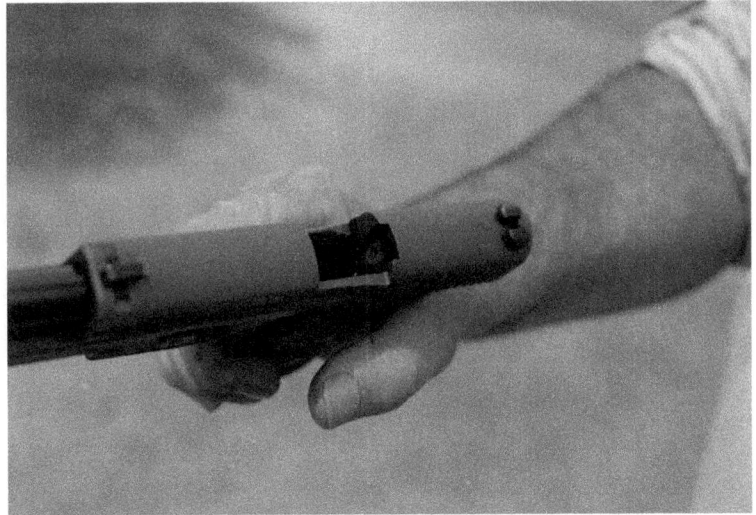

Responsible Citizens Seeking Responsible Training

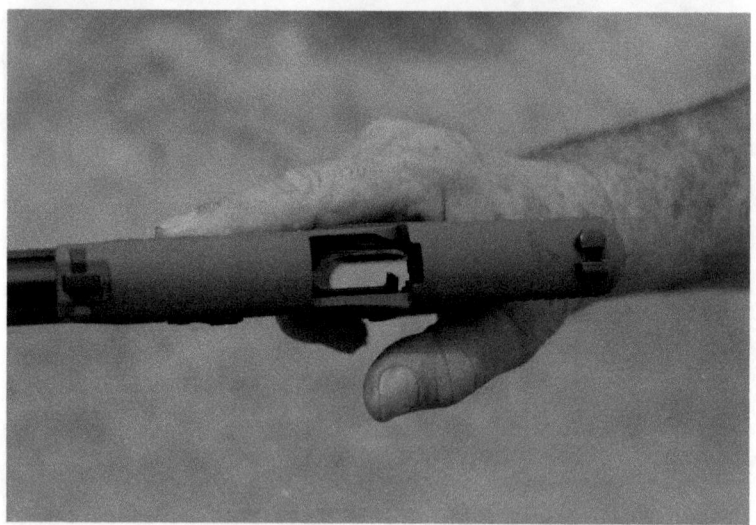

When working with others on a firing line I will also have my students conduct a "buddy check".

With the slide locked to the rear after I check it twice, show the shooter on your left or right and let them get one finial look.

Safety cannot be compromised!

There are no "Accidental" Discharges!

Negligent discharges are never acceptable.

Types of Shooting Stances and Platforms

Weaver Stance

The first component is a two-handed technique in which the shooting hand holds the pistol or revolver while the support hand wraps around the shooting hand. The shooting arm's elbow is slightly bent (almost locked out) while the support elbow is noticeably bent straight down. The shooter pushes forward with his/her shooting hand while the support hand exerts rearward pressure on the firearm. The resultant isometric tension from the support hand is intended to lessen and control muzzle flip when the firearm is fired; allowing for faster follow-up shots.

The second component is the positioning of the feet in a boxing stance, with the non-shooting side foot ahead of the shooting side foot. A person shooting right-handed will have the right foot angled out to approximately forty-five degrees to the side and to the rear at shoulder length. Most of the shooter's weight will be on the forward foot, with the forward knee slightly bent and the rear leg nearly straight. The shooter's upper torso should be leaning forward at the hips, aiming the shoulders towards the forward foot. The rear foot will help catch the force of recoil, as well as allow for rapid changes in position. The majority of the shooter's weight should be on the forward foot. Both of the shooter's knees should be slightly bent and the shooter should be bending forward at the waist as if preparing to be pushed backward.

The Weaver stance was known for putting two hands on the pistol. Jack Weaver is credited with developing this stance in the late 1950s for competitions.

The stance still works for one round, precise competition shooting.

This is not the most efficient technique for defending yourself!

Responsible Citizens Seeking Responsible Training

The Isosceles Stance

This a two-handed technique in which the dominant hand holds the pistol or revolver while the support hand wraps around the dominant hand. Both arms are held straight, locking the elbows. Viewed from above, the arms and chest of the shooter form an isosceles triangle, which gives the stance its name.

The Isosceles Stance passively absorbs the recoil of firing the handgun using the shooter's skeletal structure, rather than active muscular tension. The Isosceles Stance is a simple stance and is natural to perform under stress. Because the Isosceles Stance orients the torso of the shooter forward, it increases the usefulness of a ballistic vest compared to other shooting stances, which tend to present the less protected side of the torso.

The Modern Isosceles or Modified Isosceles

This shooting stance is a more aggressive, forward-leaning version of the Traditional Isosceles. The shooter places the shoulders forward of the hips, the feet shoulder width apart, support-side foot slightly forward, and the knees bent. These changes to posture shift the center of mass forward, helping the shooter better control recoil.

The shooter wanting to move extremely fast, or move around cover, must use the Modified Isosceles platform. The fastest shooters in the world use the Modified Isosceles Platform (Stance) is the positioning of the upper body in relation to the lower body or the feet.

For proper stance, the shooter should: Place the feet shoulder width apart. Position the non-firing foot slightly forward (normally 2 to 4 inches) of the firing foot and pointed directly at the target. Plant the firing foot (the back foot) firmly to provide balance. Use the firing foot to generate forward or lateral movement quickly.

Bend the knees slightly and lean the upper torso forward. Have 60 to 70 percent of the body weight forward to absorb the recoil of the weapon. Stand so the shoulders and head are square to the target and the head is erect.

Bending of the knees-It is important that the knees are slightly bent so the kneecap should ride over the ball of the support foot this aggressive positioning allows for extreme recoil management and quick movements.

Arm positioning- The arms must have a slight bend and work together as shock absorbers. Push arms forward until the shooting grip starts to degrade.
Head Positioning-Drop the head slightly and position the head to allow for continued use of the center of the eye.

The shooting platform must allow for movement; as well as, the expenditure of a whole magazines worth of ammunition while engaging multiple threats. The platform must not degrade and must work no matter the scenario.

A proper platform allows the shooter to drive the weapon. The shooter should quickly move the weapon, stop smoothly and crisply, from one target to the next. If the movement is a slow and easy motion, the shooter will not be as quick as required to quickly neutralize multiple threats. Lead with the Eyes when the need arises to engage multiple targets, the shooter must allow the eyes to move from one target to the next. Once the eyes have acquired the target, the weapon is pushed as aggressively as possible to become aligned with the eyes, thusly aligned with the target.

The fastest shooters in the world use the Modern or Modified Isosceles shooting stance. There is no argument that can support any other stance. The body under stress, surprised or scared, will naturally assume the Modified Isosceles stance!

Dry Fire – PRACTICE

Dry fire is the practice of practicing with an UNLOADED pistol.

Make sure to review the unloading and clearing procedures.

Practice everything that is learned. In the shooting world, practice is often referred to as "dry fire." In the Freefall world, we would always "dirt dive," and in the combat world, everything that could be was rehearsed.

It is important for the shooter to understand the building block process that is required in pistol shooting.

Dry firing is the shooters way to practice drawing, malfunction clearing, reloads, and trigger manipulation. Take practice very seriously.

I have already mentioned that "Super" Dave Harrington was the NCOIC of the marksmanship side of the house on my first trip to Range 37 at Fort Bragg for SOT and also on my second trip for SFARTEAC. I can remember that every afternoon there was a requirement to conduct dry fire training for 2 hours before we could turn in our pistols. At the time, I do not think I understood how important the dry practice was.

Later in my Special Forces career, Super Dave became a very good friend and I still remember that when he helped us get ready to teach our first Special Forces Advanced Urban Combat class, and that we needed to ensure our

Special Forces Warriors conducted a lot of dry fire. Super Dave told me he practiced 10,000 trigger manipulations for very round he fired. A technique that I have tried to emulate.

I have dry fired for years, I believe in the concept. I practice on most days when I cannot live fire. But even after years of dedicated practice, I was truly amazed while working the 2016 SHOT show for Sig.

My station was close to the demonstration stand, so I got the privilege of watching Max Michel dry fire. He was getting ready to conduct a demonstration for about 1000 people. A few days prior Max had set the world record for plate shooting and was the fastest demonstration shooter in the world! As I watched Max dry fire, he missed an emergency reload that would be required for his demonstration. He stopped and dry fired that piece of the demo until he could not get it wrong. Then he went back to practicing the entire sequence. Of course, it was another amazing demonstration.

What I have learned and have been privileged to have reaffirmed by getting to know and watch some of the best in the world is that I cannot dry fire practice too much!

Dry Firing will allow the student of shooting to get in the proper mindset, to visualize the correct methodologies and see the desired outcome. You never know when a threat will present itself and when you will be called upon to demonstrate your proficiency.

Practice all your firearms safety rules. Unload your pistol or use your red gun or airsoft gun. Designate a clear and safe area. Know your target and what is beyond it. Don't point your weapon at anything you do not want to destroy.

When learning a new technique, dry fire it before you do it live.

Some shooters do not believe that dry firing is for them, I would tell them it will only make you better!

Practice and practice safely!   Perfect practice will result in excellent execution!

I am very paranoid when I dry fire. I clear the gun, clear it again. Do not forget to remove all live ammo from the dry fire area. Ensure all magazines are clean or prepared with the inert dummy rounds.

Always have a clear down range area and make sure there is NO ONE that could be hurt.

I know people that have failed to properly unload and clear their pistol and have shot their televisions, walls and mirrors.

YOU CANNOT BE TOO SAFE

Remember that the best shooters practice through Dry Firing!

The key to successful Dry Firing is that the shooter must understand live firing and that quality is better than quantity.

Crystal clear sight picture, see the imperfections on your front sight! Feel the metal imperfections on your trigger!

This is when you train your eyes and practice perfectly, don't cheat!

Stance (Platform). Shooting Platform - The stance is designed to serve as a foundation for rapid shooting techniques. This will lay the foundation for rapid engagement of multiple targets and movement in any direction. The position should be balanced and aggressive, both mentally and physically. By gaining a good shooting platform, the shooter gains balance, stability, mobility, and a natural point of aim.

A shooting platform is simply a position. Standing, kneeling, prone, sitting, squatting, or whatever you do, all qualify. Take that position and start moving and it becomes a platform.

It's not where you put your feet; it's where you put your balance and center of gravity and how you manage recoil energy. If you are not effectively able to manage this energy, you will not shoot well.

Your Stance is a fighting stance and your fighting stance is a shooting stance. The shooting platform must allow for quick movement. The shooting platform must allow for quick follow through and reengagement of the threat. The shooting platform should lower the shooters silhouette. The shooting platform should allow for shooting and moving. The shooting platform should work naturally and does not require changes when adding assault gear, body armor or movement. Slightly bend your knees.

It is important that the knees are bent enough to allow the kneecap to ride over the toes. This will help with obtaining an aggressive posture. This will allow for a "nose over toes" alignment.

The Grip

Regardless of the grip a shooter uses, and some grips are better than others; ALWAYS ensure both thumbs are on the same side of the pistol!

Find the grip that provides the most efficient method for multiple rounds fired accurately and quickly.

Thumb over Thumb (Thumb Trap)

Thumb over thumb is taught to several agencies and I see several people that continue to use this grip. The grip does work; however, it is not efficient for multiple round engagements. This grip also leads to unwanted pistol manipulations that decrease accurate hits.

The Clam Shell

The clam shell grip is a version of a thumbs forward grip. The clam shell grip is established by placing the back of the palm together on the back-strap of the pistol.

This grip allows the thumbs to float upwards and often causes the fingers on the support hand to tighten and adversely affect the movement of the pistol during recoil.

The clam shell grip loses recoil management as the thumbs float upward and the support hand/wrist tendon is not kept tightly extended.

I was taught the **Thumbs Forward Grip.** There are other ways to hold a semi auto pistol, as previously show; but none are as effective and efficient.

This technique was developed by the OSS (founders of the US Army Special Forces and the CIA Ground Branch) in the early part of World War two. This technique was incorporated into the competition shooting world in the 1970s and has continually out performed any other technique. This is not new!

This technique will improve your grip and vastly improve your shooting ability. If the goal is to shoot both fast and accurate, this is the proper technique!

Responsible Citizens Seeking Responsible Training

Place the strong hand as high on the pistol as possible. As the strong hand slides higher, the shooter takes away the leverage that the pistol presents during recoil.

If the pistol being used has a single action type safety like a Colt 1911 or a safety decocker like a Berretta 92F or the new US Army M17/Sig320 with a manual safety the thumbs should sweep forward while establishing the grip and taking the safety off.

Place the support hand with as much of the meaty portion of the palm on the pistol grip as possible

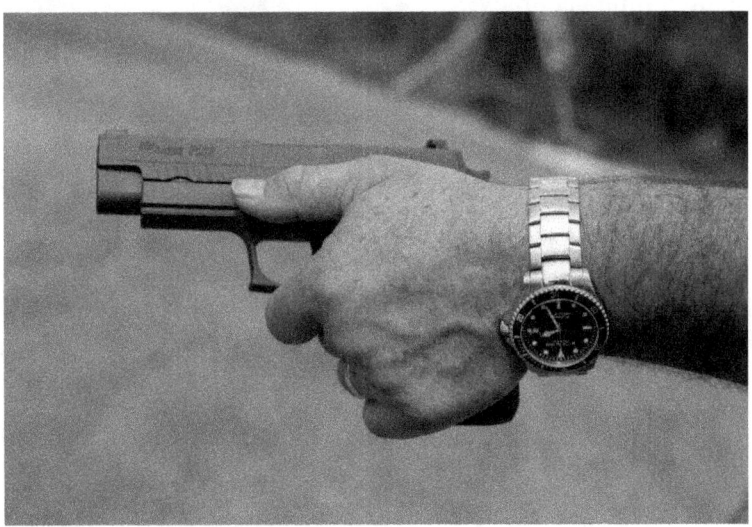

The support hand should be canted as far forward as naturally possible. Point the support thumb downrange at your target (kinesthetic aiming), it should fall naturally against the side of the pistol.

If the grip is established correctly the trigger finger should be allowed to lay the first digit finger pad on the center portion of the trigger face. The trigger finger must be slightly relaxed to allow for trigger manipulation without disturbing the sights.

DO NOT allow the index finger to slide over the front of the trigger guard. Ensure that there is no gap between the hands by pushing the palm of the support hand into the empty space.

When using this technique, the shooter will see their sights return to the center of the target much quicker. The grip must allow for the shooter to shoot extremely quickly while maintaining accuracy.

Grip is the holding of the weapon with the hand. For proper grip, the shooter should position the firing hand (strong hand) to form a fist around the handle of the pistol.

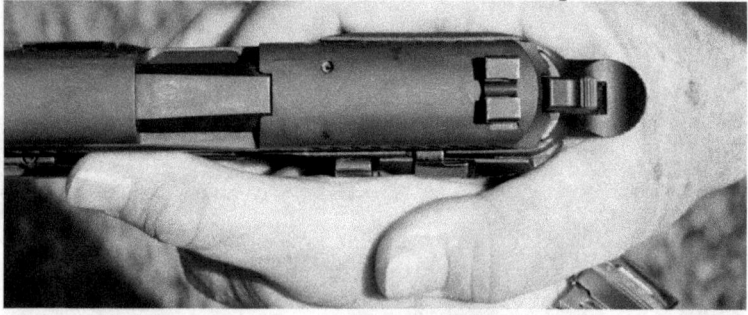

A proper Thumbs Forward grip on most Sig Sauer pistols will require the strong hand thumb to be slightly rolled to away from the pistol for a right-handed shooter to avoid "riding" the slide and preventing the pistol from locking to the rear

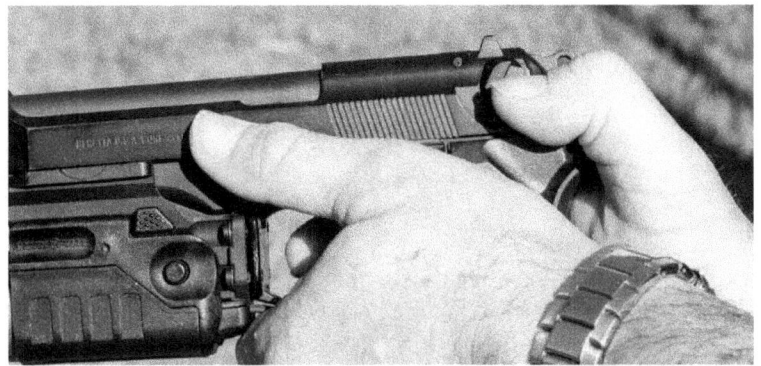

When working with a Beretta 92 style pistol with a safety/decocker the strong side thumb should push the safety forward to ensure the pistol is ready to fire.

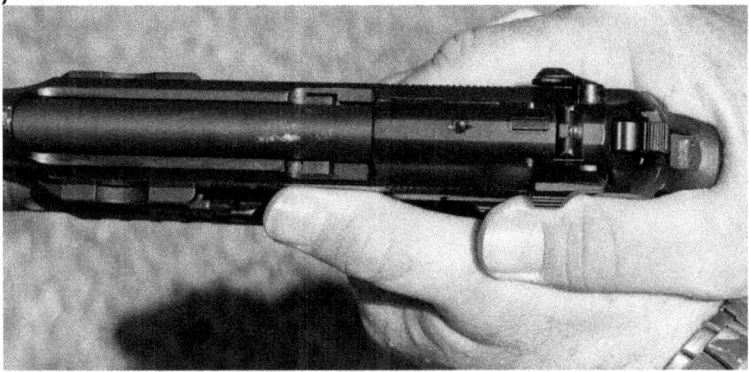

The Beretta style safety should always be swept forward, even when only used as a decocker.

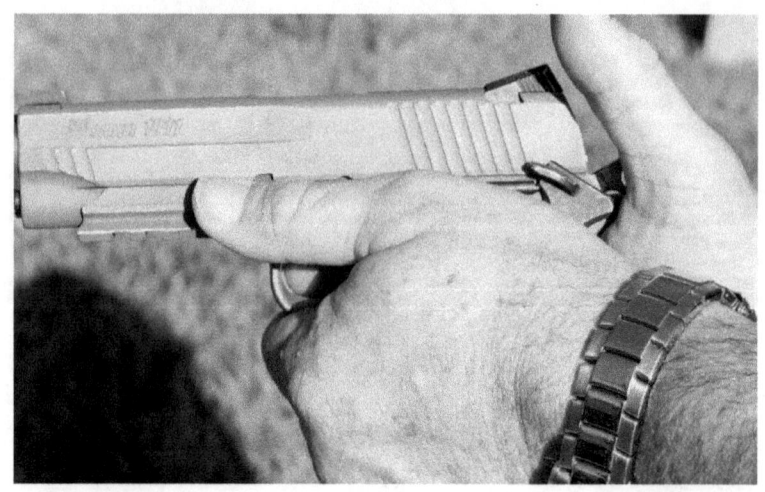

When working with 1911 style pistols the strong side thumb should be used to disengage the thumb safety.

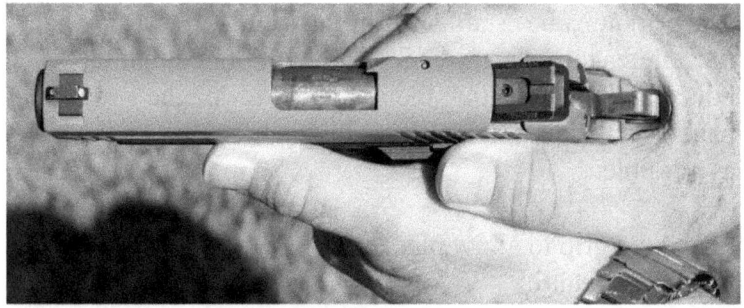

The Thumbs Forward Grip was originally designed for this style pistol! The goal is to put as much meat on the pistol as possible.

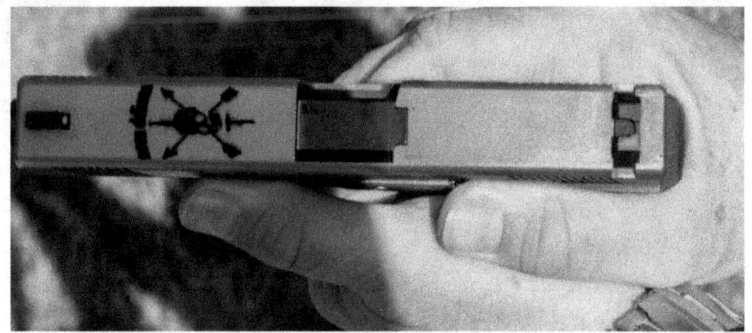

This grip works on all pistols with all hand sizes

Responsible Citizens Seeking Responsible Training

The grip must be established in **Position 1,** the strong hand must defeat any retention device incorporated into the holster. While defeating the retention device the strong hand establishes a tight grip as high on the tang of the pistol as possible.

Shape the grip to allow placement of the trigger finger for maximum control

Place the non-firing hand (support hand) to form a fist over the firing hand (strong hand). Position the non-firing thumb along the slide and the index finger of the non-firing hand (support hand) under the trigger guard, pushing up.

In order to squeeze the trigger without disturbing the sights, and to shoot quickly, the trigger finger and hand must be slightly more relaxed than the support hand. The trigger finger must be taught to squeeze without the remaining fingers applying rearward pressure.

Relax the strong hand and the trigger finger will be able to manipulate the trigger easily without disturbing the sight picture, or the rest of the shooting grip.

Responsible Citizens Seeking Responsible Training

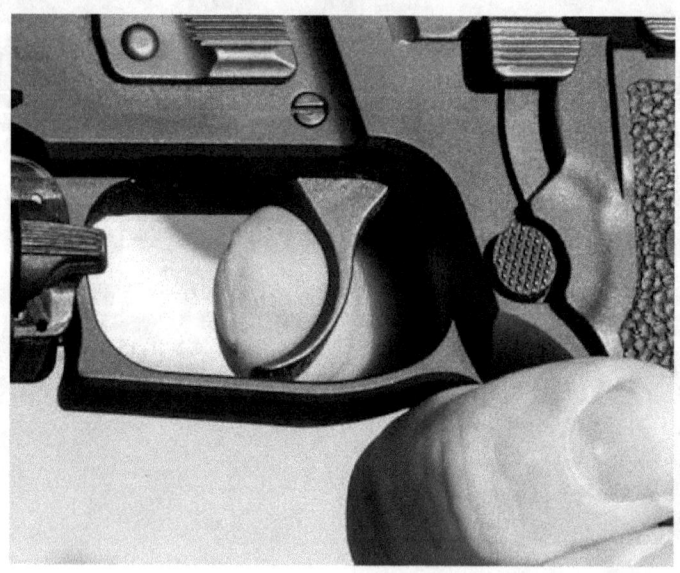

The correct finger trigger placement will generally be in the middle of the finger pad.

The pinch created by the support-hand grip causes isometric tension of the support hand to force the gun down and the upward push against the trigger guard by the index finger of the support hand. The positioning of the thumb varies from shooter to shooter, as does the grip depending on the pistol.

BIOMETRIC INDEXING will allow for the strong hand thumb to act as a pointer and aid in target acquisition. By proper placement of the thumb, the pistol sights will be acquired quicker.

The support hand also aids in the body's natural ability to bio-index.

When establishing a good and efficient grip, the support hand fingers should fit into the strong hand knuckle grooves.

A good thumbs-forward grip will allow the support hand thumb to lock out the support hand wrist tendon and point toward the target.

The support thumb should be allowed to naturally point to the target.

The support hand if opened during training should allow for the fingers to be at a 45 degree angle. The support hand fingers should also allow for the middle finger pad to rest in between the knuckles of the strong hand

If the support hand is opened and the fingers are pointing downward at a 45% angle then the shooter will know that the support hand tendon is tight and then the recoil of the pistol will be much better managed.

When the thumbs creep up, the support fingers will go from 45% to 90% and then the pistol will experience much more movement during recoil.

A proper grip will allow for several things if executed correctly. The recoil of the pistol will be much better managed. Shots will be more accurate and faster.

There are several techniques that will allow for very accurate one-shot engagements, so another quick review!

Thumb Trap allows for the thumb of the strong hand to be trapped to the side of the pistol by the support hand.

The Clam shell is a modified thumbs-forward but allows the support hand tendon to become relaxed.

Any of these grips will work for one shot accurate engagements, but if a shooter desires to improve on the current proficiency level the thumbs forward grip is a must!

If the goal is to shoot fast and accurate, the shooter must manage recoil and the thumbs forward technique is best method to use.

The proper grip will allow for follow through and recovery. Any grip, even placing the gun upside down as demonstrated above; will allow for accurate ONE-SHOT engagements!

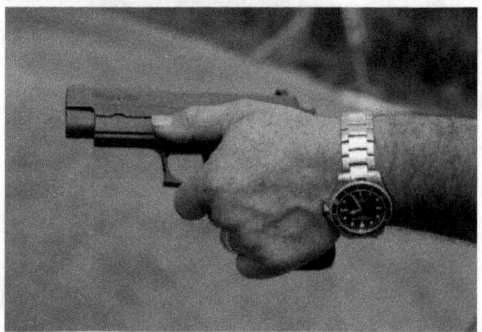

Responsible Citizens Seeking Responsible Training

PRESENTATION from the Holster, a four (4) step Draw stroke

Position 1- Position of the draw. On the count of one, move the firing hand to the holster and grasp the weapon, forming the proper grip.

The strong-arm movement should appear to be a very aggressive rear elbow strike.

Bend the non-firing arm to a 90° angle about mid-chest level, with the fingers slightly curved and joined and the thumb pointing to the target. This will form the "meet and greet" when the hands come together.

Both hands are in motion at the same time.

CONTACT BODY: The strong hand moves back, contacting the torso high on the rib cage, until poised directly over the holster. By maintaining contact with the body, the shooter can locate the weapon under stress.

Disengage any pistol retention devices. The strong hand moves straight down (maintaining contact with the body), breaking the retention as the shooting grip is established.

Responsible Citizens Seeking Responsible Training

The support hand moves towards the high center of the body to receive the drawn weapon. I prefer to conduct my meet and greet in the high chest or chin area.

The thumb is rotated towards the target and the palm is readied to accept the weapon.

Allows for the strong hand to rest on the pistol and will be the point where the grip is established. The strong hand thumb does not rest alongside the frame. It remains in a high thumb position to allow maximum contact of the support hand on the grip. (Review the Thumbs Forward Grip)

Position 2-The strong hand lifts the weapon from the holster.

It is important that the weapon is lifted as high as possible on the pectoral muscle/armpit before it is rotated towards the threat (into an extreme close quarter position).

The hands are brought together near the center-line of the body to establish a two-handed shooting grip. On the count of two, raise the weapon until it clears the holster, and with the thumb of the firing hand, disengage the safety.

Allows for the pistol to clear the holster and allows for the muzzle to start to come upward to your intended target

Position Two (2) allows for well-placed extreme close quarter shot placement in the pelvic region. This allows the shooter to engage without doing anything different in their draw stroke.

Responsible Citizens Seeking Responsible Training

Position 3- As the two-handed grip is established, the weapon is driven directly to the shooting position, i.e., eye level. Exactly where the hands come together may vary from shooter to shooter.

Variables such as physical characteristics, type and location of holster and dominant eye may cause variances in the draw stroke.

The over-riding principles are economy of motion and quickly bringing the weapon into position to fire accurate shots. One should be aggressive on the trigger.

Responsible Citizens Seeking Responsible Training

Unintentional discharges may occur in the beginning of training.

Remember when presenting the pistol, DO NOT allow the sights to go above the target.

Recoil will happen, regardless of technique. How much recoil/muzzle lift occurs will be determined by how well the grip is set.

The proper grip and stance allow the weapon to recoil consistently, with the weapon returning to alignment on target, thereby allowing rapid follow-up.

On the count of three, move the non-firing hand to meet the firing hand near the upper portion of the midsection.

A common misconception is that both hands have to be in the perfect grip, this is not true, and is almost impossible to achieve at real-life shooting speed draw requirements. The shooter should always attempt to have a perfect grip in training.

Disengage the safety at this point with the non-firing hand if unable to do so at Position 2.

Keep the weapon pointed at the target. Transfer the trigger finger from the side of the weapon to the trigger. Position three (3) is the most important position before actually firing the weapon. Position 3 is a retention position

Responsible Citizens Seeking Responsible Training

Many professionals from the field engage a threat, and then are taught to lower their muzzle and lock out their arms by assuming a low ready that allows us to see the hands. (Low Ready)

This is not part of the draw stroke. Many shooters may need to consider looking at a more efficient adult learning concept and return back to position #3 (Retention Position or Close Quarters).

This allows the shooter to return to a known shooting position rather than a totally altered position that does not allow for quick target acquisition if needed.

Position 3 should allow the shooter to have a straight strong side wrist as established on the push out. *Push-out* motion will allow the sights to remain aligned and smoothly transition from close quarters to full extension. The bore axis of your pistol is in a ready position that will allow for the shooter to begin manipulation of the trigger. Trigger manipulation will actually allow for emergency shooting from this position. Continue the engagement process until the sights have been acquired and the threat is eliminated. Prep the Trigger. Take the slack out of the trigger so that as soon as the sights stop on the desired aiming point the shot can break.

The shooter must establish the perfect grip in Position 1 by establishing a high-thumbs forward grip, the support hand should be in receiving mode. In Position 3 the shooter should have hands prepared to assume the perfect position as the weapon is pushed toward the target.

Position 3 will allow for a transition period when the trigger finger removes the slack or extra movement in the trigger as the pistol is pushed out to full extension.

Position 4- On the count of four, push the weapon out to the line of sight while removing slack from the trigger.

Achieve a sight picture and fire.

Position 4 allows for several things to happen. The safety should be disengaged. The sights should be placed on the threat. The trigger should be prepped. Taking out the trigger slack but not firing until the shooter has obtained an acceptable sight picture.

Upon firing the position will allow for follow through and trigger reset and the ability to follow up with as many rounds and needed to eliminate the threat.

Responsible Citizens Seeking Responsible Training

Working Area

In order to develop proper neurological imprinting and simplify procedures, all weapons handling skills [loading and reloading, immediate action drills (IAD's) and clearing procedures] are accomplished in a working area (control area) directly in front of the chin.

A valuable reference is the phrase "eye-muzzle-threat". When utilized properly, this position keeps the shooters head up so that the shooter can see both the threat area and their weapon at the same time.

This must be covered in basic training courses and always practiced during dry fire for detailed muscle memory.

When any manipulation of the weapon occurs it is imperative that the weapon stays between the shooter and the target.

I watch many good shooters and instructors drop the gun below the line of sight to conduct reloads and work malfunctions; this is wrong and will get you hurt!

Keep your head up! Situational awareness. Know what is happening around you at all times.

Responsible Citizens Seeking Responsible Training

BROOMSTICK DRILL

The broomstick drill will require a coach. The coach will hold a "broomstick" or target stake. I like using a cardboard target backer.

Hold the "broomstick" chest high and far enough away from the body to allow for a good high draw stroke.

BROOMSTICK DRILL

The broomstick drill will allow for the neurological imprinting of a good draw stroke. This learning technique will help to expose the *bowling* and *cast fishing* draw strokes.

Responsible Citizens Seeking Responsible Training

Loading Unloading Malfunctions

Loading

The most important difference in loading for a responsible shooter is to always try to load as though it were a speed reload, but without the speed.

The responsible shooter should always try training with the goal of making the overall shooting process better, a completely administrative loading procedure IS NOT going to help with combat or realistic shooting.

Once the magazine starts to slide into the weapon, seat it with the same vigor that would be used in a speed reload

Initial Loading - The term used for loading the weapon for daily carry, in a safe manner, while executing several steps that reduce the potential for negligent discharges and ensure that the weapon will function properly.

There are two possible weapons conditions for initial loading of the weapon- slide forward and the slide lock to the rear. Slide Forward:

Responsible Citizens Seeking Responsible Training

Draw and obtain a sight picture (pointing the weapon in a safe direction).

This is consistent with developing proper neurological imprinting on technique. Keep the finger off the trigger and outside of the trigger guard. Obviously, safety and location dictate whether a sight picture is obtained or the weapon is pointed into a safe direction only!

While the strong hand pulls the weapon into the working area, the support hand moves to the magazine pouch where the support hand index finger is placed along the entire front edge of the magazine pouch, drawing the magazine into the support hand (this technique is referred to as "indexing a magazine").

Always retrieve the magazine where it is carried every day. If you carry your spare magazine in your front or rear pocket, load from there! A free repetition, free practice to develop the required muscle memory!

Insert it into the magazine well with enough pressure to fully seat it, but not send the slide forward prematurely. Ideally the shooter should maintain focus on the threat, and glance (if needed) at the magazine into ensure it's in the mag well, then quickly refocusing on the threat once the magazine begins to seat.

These two motions are accomplished at the same time (two hands in motion).

Send the slide forward by either rotating the weapon inboard, grasping the slide, and pulling the slide briskly to the rear allowing the slide to "Sling-Shot" forward, chambering a round.

Rotating the slide to a vertical position, grasping the slide in the "power stroke" or "hand over "method (palm over the top of the slide), and pulling to the rear allowing the slide to sling shot forward, *Push* the weapon back on target after re-establishing a solid two-handed grip and immediately re-obtain another sight picture. Recover to the ready, close quarters, or position 3, finger off the trigger and outside the trigger guard.

Slide Locked to the Rear. The above procedures remain the same with the following exception: Pull the weapon back to the loading (control area) position, maintaining an "eye-muzzle-threat" or "eye-magazine well- threat" line of sight. Using the grasping grooves, pull the slide to the rear and push up on the slide stop to lock the slide back or using the slide release (lock, catch) lever to send the slide forward.

Perform a Press Check
Once the round has been chambered, maintain control of the weapon in the strong hand. The strong hand thumb will be on or beside the hammer (or slide) of the weapon. Keep the trigger finger off the trigger and outside the trigger guard. Place the thumb of the support hand on the back of the hammer or high on the tang. Curl the index finger or the index and middle finger and place them in front of the rear sight. Move the slide back just enough to see a portion of the casing through the ejection port or far enough to insert the support hand pinky to touch the brass (Low Light conditions).

Once the press check is complete, ensure the slide goes fully into battery.

Do not rely on **Loaded Chamber Indicators**. Loaded chamber indicators can give a false reading or may not work well with gloves or if the weapon is very dirty or there is debris under the extractor. Never trust these indicators. De-cock (if applicable)

In the case of double action only pistols or weaker shooters, press checks may be accomplished by using the grasping grooves to pull the slide back. There are numerous techniques for performing a press check, this procedure is preferred due to efficiency and economy of motion.

The 1911 press is often used, but it is very important not to place fingers in front of the muzzle.

Shooters should use "soft hands" on the weapon when performing immediate action procedures or reloads. This ensures these skills are performed correctly and the problem is corrected, not compounded (i.e., sending the slide forward prematurely by slamming the magazine into the magazine well.)

There are pistols designed with an auto load function. I have found that I cannot trust this feature every time. If your pistol does not have an auto load feature and the slide goes forward on loads or reloads ensure you are hitting the rear of the magazine well and not the bottom of the magazine. If the correct procedure is in place and the slide goes forward, have your pistol looked at by a certified armorer.

Unloading- Unloading should be done as follows:

Draw and obtain a sight picture, ensuring the weapon is pointed in a safe direction (down range).
Remove the finger from the trigger guard. Bring the weapon to the loading position and tilt slightly.

Remove the magazine and place it in the pocket. Using the "Push-Pull" method, use the grasping grooves of the slide

Responsible Citizens Seeking Responsible Training

and rack the slide back with sufficient force to eject any live round from the chamber.

You should visually observe the round ejecting. At this point the weapon should be unloaded.
Ensure the muzzle remains pointed down range.
Work the slide 2-3 times. Grasp the slide and lock it to the rear.

Visually and physically inspect the chamber and magazine well to ensure that it is unloaded.
Look away and then look back. Check it twice! (CIT).
Release the slide, de-cock (if appropriate) and holster.
Unloading for the left-handed shooter is the same. This procedure should mimic the clearing procedure that the shooter has been using.

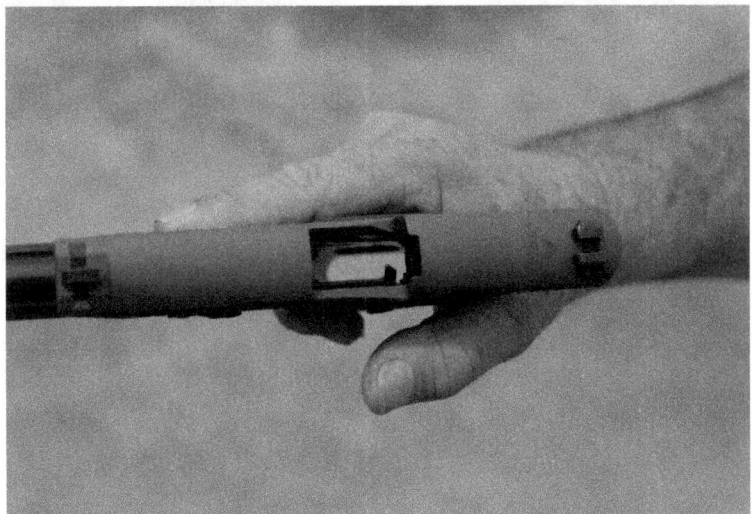

Responsible Citizens Seeking Responsible Training

Reloads

Emergency or Slide Lock Reload. This term is used when you have fired all the rounds in the magazine of the weapon and the slide is locked to the rear.

In a lethal force confrontation, this constitutes an emergency.

Remove the trigger finger from the trigger guard.

Two hands are in motion at the same time. With the strong hand, depress the magazine release as you bring the weapon into the loading position and can't the weapon slightly sideways (grip inboard) to receive fresh magazine.

There are two methods of depressing the magazine release.

Responsible Citizens Seeking Responsible Training

The left-handed person will probably depress the magazine release with the trigger finger unless the weapon is a configured with a left-hand magazine release.

The right-handed shooter will probably use the thumb of the firing hand.

DO NOT attempt to catch the empty magazine. Let it hit the ground. The empty magazine will fall free quicker if the weapon is still straight up and down and not in a vertical position. Using the strong hand thumb/finger puts the support hand in motion to the magazine pouch sooner than using the support thumb to press the magazine release button.

With the support hand index finger along the entire front edge of the magazine pouch, draw the magazine into the support hand ("indexing a magazine"). Practice the same way the pistol was loaded. Get the magazine from where you carry it! If you carry the magazine in a pocket, reload from there!

Insert it into the magazine well with enough pressure to fully seat it, but not send the slide forward prematurely.

Once the magazine starts in the well, refocus on the threat. Allow slide to go forward! There are three methods that may be used

Responsible Citizens Seeking Responsible Training

SLIDE RELEASE (lock, catch) lever to send the slide forward. During high-stress situations where finding the small slide stop may be difficult. This is a technique that requires practice.

SCISSORS The fore finger and thumb of the support hand are used to grab the grasping grooves. (Grasping Grooves method may also be preferred during high-stress situations where finding the small slide stop may be difficult). When using this technique, the pistol must be rotated in toward the centerline of the body.

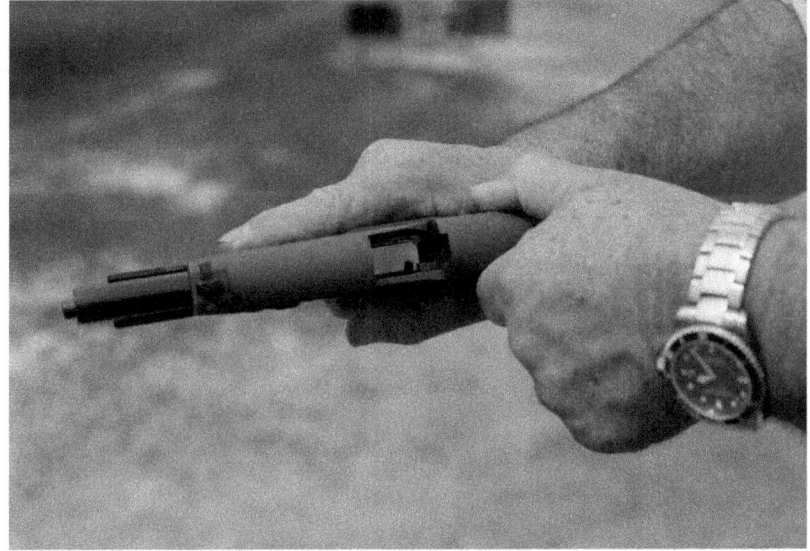

POWER STROKE the support hand comes over the top of the slide and a reverse grip is used to grasp the grasping grooves. If used the shooter must ensure that the support hand does not cover up ejection port because this may induce malfunctions.

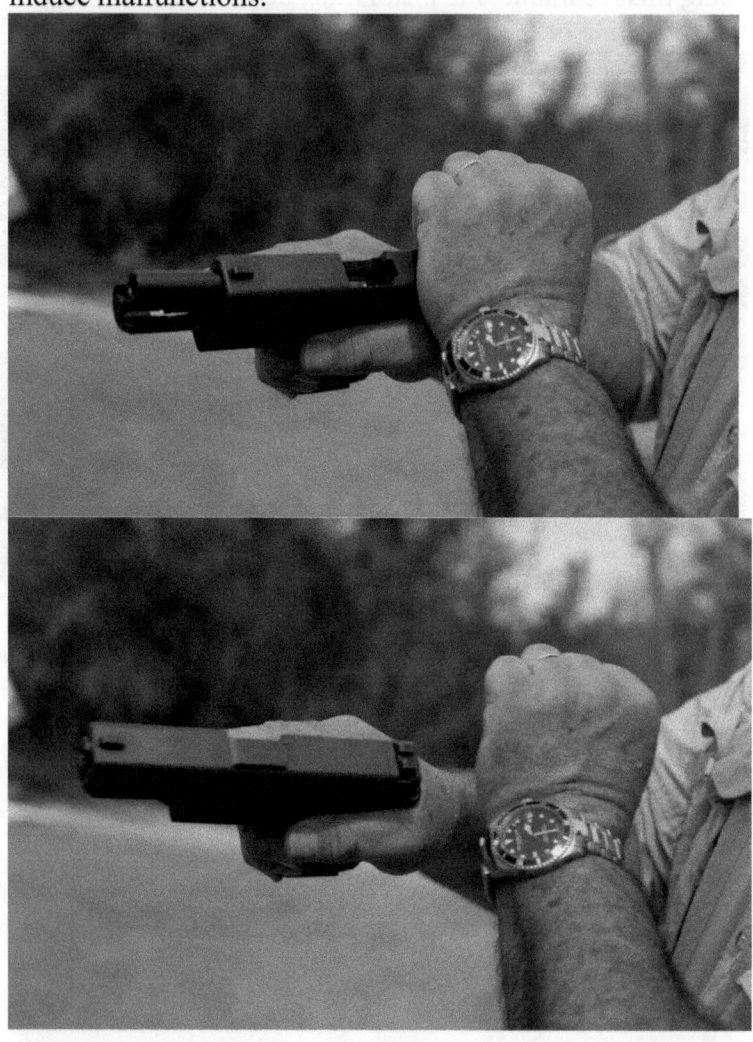

As an added technique, draw the magazine from the support side pocket to replicate an emergency reload AFTER a magazine exchange or supplemental ammunition capacity.

Bring the weapon back up on target.

Tactical Reload without Retention or Speed Reload.

Speed reload are the same as a slide lock reload with the exception of not having to release the slide to go forward. The speed reload is used when speed is of the essence and the shooter has the ability to back and retrieve magazines

Tactical Reload with Retention-Magazine Exchange.
Seek Cover if possible. Use proper magazine grasping technique, the same technique that would be used for normal reloads. Secure a fully prepared magazine.

Create space in the support hand to allow for the partial magazine to fall on top of the full magazine. This technique will allow the shooter to always maintain a secure grip on partial and full magazines.

Once the partial magazine is free from the weapon, rotate the full magazine into the magazine well seat it with a purpose. As you seat the magazine rotate the hand that is holding the partial so that you have the power needed to properly seat the new magazine. Place the partially-loaded magazine in your pocket or pouch, preferably behind any full magazines.

If the procedure is to place the magazine in the pocket (not in a pouch), then "pocket reloads" should be an alternate procedure to standard emergency reloads from a pouch.

An alternate method, considering gross motor skills under conditions of stress, would be to have the shooter remove the magazine from the weapon and place it in their pocket, then insert a fully-loaded magazine from their pouch.

Considering the level of emergency/tactical reloads for muscle memory, this method may prove to be the most efficient manner of conducting a magazine exchange.

Primary Malfunction Procedures (Tap-Rack-Ready).

Malfunction of the gun is when you pull the trigger and nothing happens.

Take the finger off the trigger and place it alongside the frame before you TAP the bottom. *TAP* the bottom of the magazine to ensure that it is seated (locked into the bottom of the pistol). At the same time, the pistol should be brought back into your working area. The gun should be turned so that the magazine is facing your center line.

Responsible Citizens Seeking Responsible Training

RACKING is accomplished by quickly pulling the slide to the rear. Turn the gun so that the slide is facing your center line and the magazine is facing out. Let the slide just SLAM forward. This can be accomplished by using the slide lock lever, pinching the REAR serrations (Sling Shot Technique) or coming over the top. (Power Stroke)

READY is when the weapon is removed from the secured area with the operable hand and now is ready to resume threat engagement or active threat cover measures. Reassess, to decide if you need to shoot again

Secondary Malfunctions/ Remedial Action (Rip-Work-Reload- Ready). This action is required when immediate malfunction recovery did not work. *RIP*: Remove the source of feed (Magazine). The shooter may lock the slide to the rear; however, this is not always needed. *Work:* All prior processes from primary malfunctions. Cycle the slide until the shooter is certain the ammunition is dislodged. *Reload*

Alternate Remedial Action works well when simply holding the magazine release button and cycling the slide. The slide, its contents and obstructions should fall free.

Remedial m alfunction procedures will be need to clear a stovepipe, double feed, stuck case or failure to extract. The shooter may experience other malfunctions caused by broken parts or due to the cleanliness of the weapon.

Fix it and get back in the fight

It should be pointed out to the shooter that, on occasion, it may be necessary to lock the slide to the rear before clearing a "failure to extract" malfunction.

The easy way to remember how to fix the gun, unload it, clear it and then reload it. This must just be done in a quick manner!

Use the method to hook the rear sight on a firm object and push down on the weapon, thereby allowing the slide to go to the rear.

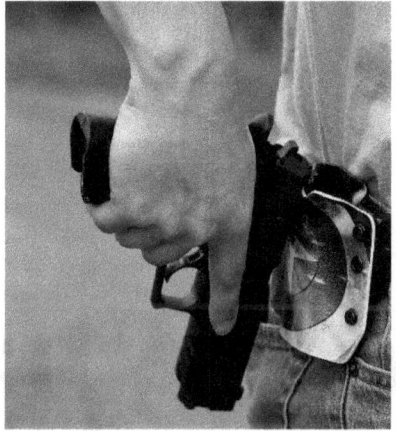

Then using the right thumb or left index finger, push up on the slide catch and allow the slide to lock back. Once the slide has been locked back, proceed with the method of one hand rip-work-tap-rack-ready.

If the shooter is using a Glock or another weapon system where the magazine floor plates are not easy to hook onto something, they can push in on the magazine release and in a forceful downward motion; hit their forearm onto their thigh.

They must ensure that the wrist and magazine are away from the leg when performing this technique in order for the magazine to be able to drop from the magazine well.

While this option cannot be ignored, the majority of malfunctions and double feed FAILURE TO EXTRACT problems can be cleared with RIP-WORK-RELOAD-READY

Responsible Citizens Seeking Responsible Training

See What You Are Shooting

KYLE A. BARRINGTON

Sighting Package is an all-encompassing way of referencing a sight picture that will allow the shooter to obtain the required amount of accuracy to eliminate the threat.

As shooters we must remember that the need for speed is crucial. The shooter must beat his adversary to the draw, but only if the required accuracy is there to eliminate the threat.

The shooter must use as much of the sighting package as required, whether that sight package uses iron front and rear, iron front only, optic or laser. The shooter must understand that as tactical distances increase the more precise the sight package must become to obtain and ensure accuracy.

The Sighting Package must be the method that best allows the shooter to accurately engage the threat at the given distance.

Every shooter has their preferences and nobody has the definitive choice in what the best sight picture is. When it comes down to making a decision, the trained shooter must weigh multiple considerations when choosing the desired sight package that will allow for accurate shots to be placed in the threat at various distances, lighting conditions and environmental considerations.

Sight Alignment is the action of aligning the weapon sights. Center the front sight blade into the rear sight notch.

This is one of the most important of the fundamentals. The sights are placed on a pistol to be used! Proper alignment is required to ensure proper round placement and accountability.

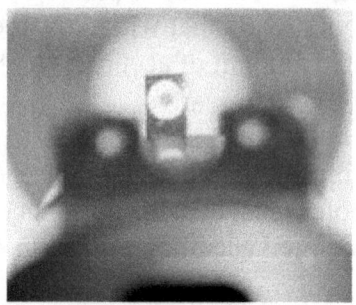

During training the shooter should work to achieve the best sight alignment possible as they go through the basic presentation drills. Once tested during a speed drill the shooter will see and understand that they can quickly acquire and align the sights while presenting the pistol.

Sight Picture The sight picture is the correlation between the front sight blade, the rear aperture, and the target as seen by the shooter. Center the top edge of the blade in the rear aperture.

Place the top edge of the blade in the center of the largest visible mass of the target (disregard the head for centering on a target and use the center of the torso. The eye will naturally center the entire target, this may not be a true center mass of the intended target).

The sight picture is the correlation between the front sight blade, the rear aperture, and the target.

The eye can focus on only one object at a time at different distances. Therefore, the last focus of the eye is always on the front sight. When the shooter sees the front sight clearly, the rear sight and target are out of focus but aligned.

Sights are placed on a gun for a reason, use them. When you are at the range always strive for the perfect sight picture. When conducting dry fire exercises, get the best sight picture possible.

Kinesthetic Skills and Visual Skills. Shooting fast and accurately also involves using kinesthetic skills with visual skills in tandem. "the body points but the eyes verify." When trained correctly, these two systems blend synergistically into performance greater than either one can do alone.
Sights are a visual verification of skeletal alignment.

Sometimes you need this verification, oftentimes you do not. The shooter must learn to bring the gun up with the sights already aligned; using kinesthetic awareness to train the reflex until it is ingrained into "muscle memory." This must then be stress conditioned to ensure reliable performance under duress.

Using kinesthetic skills with visual skills is not a 50/50 relationship. At closer ranges, kinesthetic skills dominate with vision supporting. Target focused shooting tends to place the emphasis on using kinesthetic alignment only with the eye merely used to bring the gun on target.

The problem with this is that there are many other processes in play that tend to cause problems with holding this kinesthetic alignment and will degrade the precision of the shot being fired.

This is why we use vision to help maintain the alignment and keep the gun on target, especially if the shooter or the target is moving. In the mid-ranges, vision needs to monitor more closely to ensure the sights are where they belong and not moving all over.

Responsible Citizens Seeking Responsible Training

At longer ranges, more traditional sight focus is used to ensure the hit. Soft sight focus, hard sight focus; use the sight picture that you need to get the accurate hit. Do not sacrifice your acceptable accuracy.

To shoot well with this type of focus at speed, the shooter must be able to hold the sights aligned by feel (kinesthetic awareness) as they shoot and also be able to process what they are seeing without looking at it with a hard focus.

Acceptable sight picture. In a tactical shooting style, the need for speed is crucial. The shooter must beat his adversary to the draw, but only if the required accuracy is there to eliminate the threat.

Normally the shooter would concentrate to make sure the front and rear sight are perfectly aligned correctly. The front sight should still be located between the rear sight notches, however; this is not necessary at closer ranges.

Two elements of accurate shooting that cannot be argued: You must point the muzzle at the target. You must manipulate the trigger without adding any additional movement to the muzzle.

In order to ensure that your muzzle is pointed at the target, you must use your sights. Holding a correct sight picture on target is a noble goal, but we all know that everyone shakes.

Always attempt to perfectly practice, look for the level of focus and sight alignment that allows for the best chance of success.

If the muzzle is pointed at the target when the shot is fired, the bullet will hit the target.

In gun-fighting, as well as in competition, the goal should be to locate the target, get the gun on the target, and keep the gun on the target while you fire the shot and keep the gun in proper alignment, allow for rapid recoil; recovery and place a follow up shot if needed. What you see in accomplishing this can vary in great detail depending upon the difficulty of the shot.

There are five distinct levels of focus in regards to speed and distance:

This is always a point of contention. I do know that with proper training you can see your sights. A trained shooter will be able to focus on the sights and achieve accurate hits at speed!

If you work at seeing your sights during any type of practice your sights will be there when you need them!

When at the range you must practice everything at 100%.

I tell my students all the time, you have to know what a "10" looks like before you can settle for a "2". If you know what a perfect sight package should look like, under duress you will know what you can settle for.

Constantly, "studies" are being quoted about how you can't see your sights under stress or when your heart rate goes above a certain level.

It has been proven again and again over the years that, with correct training, you CAN see what you need to see to make fight-stopping hits under these circumstances.

To accomplish the goal of seeing your sights in a gunfight or under stress, always practice getting the best sight picture that you can no matter the distance. Remember perfect practice!

Single threat at extreme close range with an extremely fast hit -no directed focus on sights or target. The shooter may be aware of sights when they arrive (on target), but the shot is by total body feel. Remember, I am a "use the sights" guy. Practice getting a perfect sight picture during practice and dry fire work, then under stress the sights will be aligned where you need them to be!

Multiple targets at extreme close range – correct gun and body alignment (index point) on first target. Sights may or may not be in peripheral vision. Once the index is confirmed, gun just appears wherever the shooter looks. If focus is on targets, look through the sights.

The most common focus for standard shooting times and distances - Shifting focus from the target back to the sights. Closely spaced targets at a greater distance - Focus on the front sight until you see it lift, extremely difficult shot at distance or small target – aware of continual relationship between trigger pressure and sight movement.

Float the dot - Shoot the shot. The idea, and terminology, was originally used for older shooters who were having trouble focusing on the front sight and establishing a good sight picture.

Floating the dot indicates there will be some acceptable movement of the sights on the target, the shooter simply needs to focus on the front sight dot on the center of the target. After you've achieved that visual dot on the center of your target, you can then manipulate the trigger to shoot the shot without moving the dot off the intended target.

This same concept could be utilized with red-dot sights. Simply put, whether it's iron sights or a red-dot sight, shooters can use the same methods, terminology and natural abilities to simplify the shooting process and have immediate success.

Red dots of any type to including EMR or Sig Romeo 1 needs to be zeroed for a certain distance. Take the time to know where your dot and bullet will meet up! At distance know your offset. I believe that the pistol optic will do for the pistol as it did for the rifle.

Peripheral Vision Shooting or "Soft Focus" Sighting is part of sighted fire systems where we see the sight or sights without directly focusing with a hard focus on the front site itself. Soft focus shooting is sometimes called "Target Focus." This is a misnomer. Target focus may happen when the shooter focuses on the target due to Sympathetic Nervous System activation. What you need to see at very close ranges to make a good centerline hit is different from what you need to see at five to seven yards. What you need to both feel and see for a precise hit on the centerline of the body is different from throwing the gun out hoping the aim is true. What this means is that you will need to come back toward the front sight and sight alignment to be able to see what you need to see to make the hit.

To shoot well with this type of focus at speed, you must be able to hold the sights aligned by feel (kinesthetic awareness) as you shoot and be able to process what you are seeing without looking at it with a hard focus.

Soft focus shooting techniques have been used since firearms were first invented and were used in archery long before that. With the advent of high-speed competitive shooting, we have been using soft focus sighting techniques for more than three decades now. Soft focus sighting techniques can be (and have been) used very successfully in lethal force situations. They have been used in combat and hunting long before that.

In order to best use soft focus techniques successfully in stress conditions, you must be able to:
Bring the weapon to the target with the sights already aligned. Task focus on seeing the appropriate sight picture well enough to make the hit.

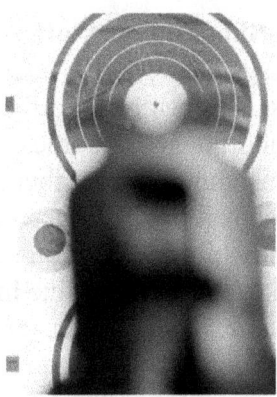

Point shooting is unsighted fire. In very limited practice it may work, but the time wasted trying to establish the perfect place to hold the weapon and still get accurate hits on target will be better used in a structured firearms training block training the shooter to use the sights.

In traditional shooting training, one is taught to focus on the front sight, keep it centered in the rear notch and let the rear sight and target become blurred as we press the trigger without unduly disturbing the sight alignment or sight picture.

Under deadly-force, close-range shooting conditions, some believe it becomes increasingly difficult to gain a true target focus on the front sight. Some folks have simply attempted to switch to point shooting, which relies on a kinesthetic alignment of the weapon with the target with vision helping to "steer" the gun on target, old west style.

The trouble with point shooting is that there are other physical processes that can interfere with getting good, fight-stopping hits. What can be done on the range, without duress, may be quite different than what can be obtained under gunfight conditions when shooting from hip.

Most instructors fail to understand that by locking the support wrist and pointing the support side and firing hand thumb with the correct support hand bio indexing the shooter is enhancing the sights of the gun. Now the shooter is actually AIMING the pistol in at least three complimentary ways!

As a Responsible Shooter, you must see your sights on every shot. The shooter is responsible for every round and must account for the impact of all rounds

Instructors that fail to recognize the multiple complimentary sighting enhancements often gravitate to "Point Shooting." As responsible gun handler's, we cannot, nor can instructors allow or teach their students, not use their sights in an attempt to use unsighted fire.

Responsible firearms owners are responsible for every round. As responsible citizens we must not forget why we are training and what we are planning to accomplish. As a

Responsible Citizens Seeking Responsible Training

Responsible Shooter, you must see your sights on every shot. You must account for the impact of every round. The rounds must impact the desired target.

Once the shooter masters the idea of seeing the sights as they move around the target and on follow through awaiting realignment before starting the next trigger manipulation, the shooter will become much more proficient.

The most important goal of tactical shooting must be hitting the target in the acceptable hit zone. We need speed; however, putting a round inside the desired zone is the primary mission.

Remember we are not discussing contact shooting engagements to include close quarters and extreme close quarters shooting. These types of engagements do not require the use of sights for the initial shots simply because the shooter is touching or almost touching the target; HOWEVER, follow up shots should require movement and the use of the sights to ensure shot placement!

Bottom line is use the sights as much as needed to make an accurate shot. Kinesthetic and peripheral awareness of the weapon are integral to tactical shooting at close distances. As the distance is increased, more focus (on the sights) must be attained to ensure accuracy.

Trigger Manipulation

Responsible Citizens Seeking Responsible Training

Trigger Control. Trigger control is the action of applying pressure to the trigger when firing the weapon.

Trigger control -Manipulating the trigger in a way that allows fast and accurate shooting. In order to ensure fast, precise hits, you must learn to manipulate the trigger with minimal disturbance of the sights on target. How fast you manipulate the trigger depends on the distance to the target, the size of the target, and the pistol you have chosen.

Regardless of ability, the shooter must learn to press and release the trigger at the same consistent speed from start to finish, using RHYTHM to assist under stressful conditions.

When first learning double-action trigger control, the shooter should pause for a moment while settling into an aiming area (a minimum arc of movement). When fired in the double-action mode, the trigger squeeze is between 9.5 and 16.5 pounds. The shooter should acquire a sight picture and then continue to apply smooth, even trigger pressure to the rear and fire.

For single-action trigger control, the shooter should remove slack from the trigger while raising the weapon to the target. The shooter should apply the initial pressure to the trigger. The trigger squeeze of the SA/DA pistol when fired in the single-action mode is generally between 4.0 and 6.5 pounds. The shooter should settle into an aiming area, acquire the sight picture, and then apply a positive increase in pressure on the trigger smoothly and evenly to the rear without interruption. After completing the trigger pull, the shooter should release the trigger without losing contact between the trigger finger and the trigger, then remove the slack to prepare to fire again. Throughout the entire trigger squeeze, the shooter should concentrate on the front sight only.

In other words, double action is twice as hard as single action. The first shot will always be double action. All following shots will be single action.

Trigger Finger. In order to better isolate the trigger, you must first have control of the handgun as well as have proper balance. A proper grip allows the hands and the handgun to move as a unit, without slipping, through the recoil cycle. Proper balance allows the body to relax and compensate for the effects of recoil without tensing up or moving. The proper balance for shooting is with the center of gravity slightly forward.

Trigger finger placement is crucial to successfully manipulating the trigger without disturbing the sights.

The first concept to understand is that the shooter must isolate the action of the trigger finger. Grip tension stays constant once the grip is set. Once the grip is set, only the trigger finger moves. The trigger must be pressed straight to the rear and not pushed or pulled to one side. One of the first skills to degrade under stress is trigger control. One of the biggest problems facing shooters is learning how to control and manipulate the trigger under tight time limits and stress, both in qualification courses and on the street.

Trigger control is composed of two parts—mental control and physical manipulation. On the mental side, control of emotions and arousal/anger comes into play. On the physical side, learning how to manipulate the trigger correctly keeps us in control at higher rates of shooting speed.

The arousal level necessary for fast precise shooting is a lot lower than that needed for most physical confrontations. I refer to this type of arousal as "calm or cold aggression." You are definitely determined, confident and focused; you just need to stay a lot calmer while doing so.

Trigger Manipulation Concepts. No matter how you choose to manipulate the trigger, the number one thing you must learn to do is to isolate the action of the trigger finger. This is part mental control and part physical manipulation. Two things make this difficult. The shooter must deal with noise and recoil at the end of the trigger press. This leads to anticipation of recoil and noise and a subsequent flinching response while manipulating the trigger. The faster you go, the greater your tendency to move other fingers while you manipulate the trigger.

Dry Fire is practicing with your **UNLOADED WEAPON** or even an airsoft or training weapon to become and stay proficient with certain techniques before expending ammunition. Dry Fire will allow the shooter to notice some of the nuances that may not be recognized during live fire. For example, while working Dry Fire trigger manipulation drills, the shooter can hear the mechanical resetting of the trigger. Dry fie is an invaluable tool for trigger manipulation drills that require proper sight alignment.

Most instructors have a predetermined amount of trigger finger engagement required to make the shooter successful. THIS IS SIMPLY WRONG. The trigger finger must be placed on the trigger where it is comfortable and allows for a smooth trigger pull. The weapon was not designed with each shooters hand in mind. Finger placement will always be dictated by the size of the shooters hands, no matter the pistol type.

Proper trigger finger placement should allow for the trigger to be manipulated straight to the rear at a constant speed without disturbing the sights. Generally, the finger pad is centered between the tip of the finger and the first knuckle.

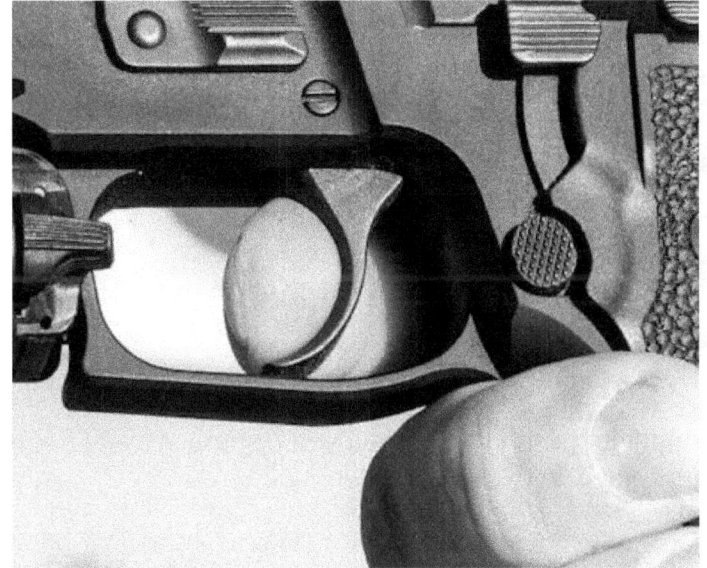

Too much finger and the impact will be pulled toward the strong hand;

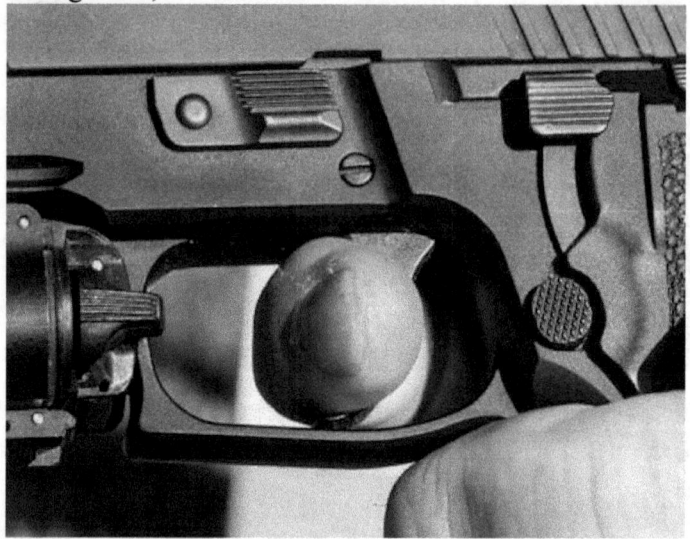

too little finger and the impact will be pushed away from the strong hand.

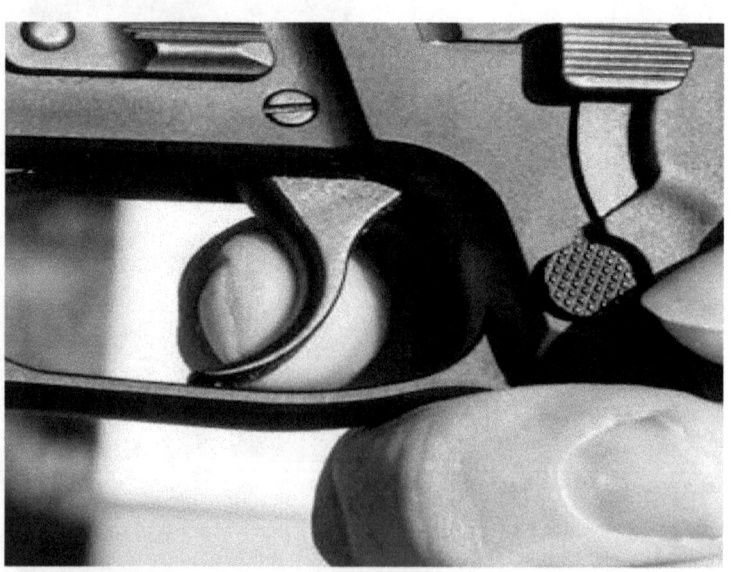

Follow-through is the action the shooter takes after firing the shot. The shooter should continue to maintain concentration on proper sight alignment even after firing the shot. Consciously attempting to keep all control factors applied through the break of the shot, provides a surprise shot break with no reflexes of anticipation to disturb sight alignment. The shooter must ensure that the sights are watched throughout the firing sequence, which includes the hammer or striker igniting the primer, the burning powder launching the bullet, the bullet hitting the target, as the weapon comes out of battery, the slide moves to the rear and another round is fed into the chamber as the disconnect or clicks and the sights now come to rest back on the target. A skilled shooter should recognize and be able to call their shot even before the bullet has time to make it to the target.

The shooter must recognize that follow through is an essential part of shooting due to the unarguable fact that multiple accurate shots must be rapidly placed.

Recovery is the process of returning the weapon to the original holding position in the center of the aiming area and securing a natural point of aim. The shooter should recover as quickly as possible. Take the recoil straight back through the shoulder acting as a shock absorber. Resume the sequence of applying the fundamentals immediately for the next shot the instant he fires the weapon.

Accurate hits as fast as possible. During training the shooter should work to achieve the perfect sight picture as they go through the basic presentation drills. After multiple practices of a speed drill, the shooter should see and understand that they can quickly acquire and align the sights while presenting the pistol. Practice often, and always strive to obtain a hard sight focus.

With correct training, the shooter CAN see what they need to see to make fight-stopping hits under these circumstances. A responsible shooter should make every effort to see the sights for every shot and use as much sight picture as required to make accurate hits. The shooter is responsible for the impact of every round. The shooter needs to develop speed. Put as many rounds in the acceptable level of accuracy as needed to eliminate the threat.

Controlled Pairs -two shots and three sight pictures. A controlled pair is the next step to firing multiple accurate shots. In other words, have one more site picture than you do shots. The shooter should look through the sights with both eyes open while focusing on the target (adversary). The sight should be coming into alignment as the pistol is smoothly brought in line with the target line and pressed towards the target. The sequence of events should be as follows: As the weapon pushes forward toward the threat, the trigger is starting to move rearward. Sights align, wrists lock, the sight alignment verified, the shot breaks. To shoot well with this type of focus at speed, the shooter must be able to hold the sights aligned by feel (kinesthetic awareness) as they shoot and also be able to process what they are seeing without looking at it with a hard focus.

Multiple shots-Always one more sight picture than shot like controlled pairs. Multiple-shots is a series of controlled pairs. Manipulate the trigger as fast as your grip will allow for recovery. Remember it is imperative to always see the front sights.

Speed/Flash Sight picture. This technique is a way to get your sights immediately on target with a lot of hits on target... not necessarily bull's-eye hits. With a Flash Sight Picture shooting at close distances, you should be able to land hits in a 10-inch target almost every time, even if your Front Sight is not perfectly aligned

Remember that a simple and extremely effective sight picture that has been developed for the aged-eye shooters (those in bifocals and trifocals) has become the standard sight picture for most mature students. It is recommended that a dot on the front sight and the widest notch available for the type of rear sight to be used. This allows the shooter to use the eye's natural ability to center round objects in square openings with incredible precision quickly.

As the shooter brings the firearm up to eye level to shoot with the target in view, they should immediately and very definitely shift total focus from the target to the FRONT SIGHT of the gun... ONLY on the FRONT SIGHT.

The proper technique involves seeing the front sight very early in the draw stroke. You should be TOTALLY FOCUSING on the very TOP of the FRONT SIGHT and see all its nooks and crannies, scratches and serrations.

When the front post is somewhere (anywhere) in between the rear sights– note you are NOT trying to precisely position the Front Sight vertically and horizontally in alignment with the Rear Sight.

Press the trigger when the front sight meets the blurry target in the background. The Front Sight blade may be slightly off right or left or high or low, but remember that

Responsible Citizens Seeking Responsible Training

this technique relies on many hits to the target, rather than on all bullseye hits.

The Rear Sights are blurry, but you only see that with your peripheral vision because the eye cannot clearly focus on more than one object at different distances at the same time. If the target and rear sights are both blurry, you have successfully focused on ONLY the front sight and are using the FSP technique. (Flash Sight Picture)

The key is making sure the trigger press, hand, and finger movement do not move the front sight off the target. At minimum distance, the grip (wrist locked and firm, high on the back strap) and trigger press (smooth, consistent, no stop-and-go straight to the rear) are the most important fundamentals.

Front sight or using a flash sight picture is only effective at limited distances.

Flash Sight Picture shooting is different from POINT-SHOOTING (PS). PS is a very controversial and debated issue. PS is the ability of a shooter to be able to hit a target WITHOUT AIMING with the Front or Rear Sights at all… to naturally point at a target

Natural Point of Aim. Natural Point of Aim is where the shooter naturally points the weapon. Injuries may affect the body's ability to naturally "aim".

Find the natural point of aim: With eyes closed, where does the shooter naturally point? Over time, the Natural point of aim may change. The main purpose of identifying and potentially correcting natural point of aim is to make shots with both accuracy and precision. You will have to adjust shooting stance to better incorporate the ability to naturally point.

To achieve natural point of aim, the shooter settles into position while not looking through the sights. Some shooters actually close their eyes, but this can upset the natural maintenance of balance because the brain uses visual cues to help stay in balance. The shooter looks through the sights only after ensuring the position is comfortable and the firearm is resting in the stance with minimal muscle tension. If the sights are not resting on the desired point of impact, the shooter adjusts the position by repeating the same steps until the sights rest on the target. After achieving a comfortable and natural position, if the sights are not on the target, the shooter adjusts his stance (moves his feet) until the sights are on target. The arm, head and body position do not change; when standing only the feet are moved to bring the sights onto target

Moving With Your Pistol

Training Distances: Many agencies and organizations I train are often convinced that gunfights take place at close range, so there is no need to practice at any distance greater than 10 yards. I disagree! The practice at greater distances ensures that the basics are being performed to perfection on demand.

It is possible with practice to engage man sized targets out to several hundred yards. Increase your training distances to 50 yards, 100 yards or greater on occasion. Hitting steel at 100 lets the shooter know that they truly understand manipulating the trigger from front to rear without disturbing the sights! Test yourself!

Target Identification- Lighting conditions do play a critical role in proper identification. Training target identification, movement, and timed decision making, along with correcting errors in judgment, have proven to be highly effective in reducing "friendly on friendly" shootings.

Threat / no Threat. Threat is a declaration of an intention or determination to inflict punishment, injury, etc., in retaliation for, or conditionally upon, some action or course; menace: Shoot/No Shoot situations must be analyzed as rapidly as possible.

For the proper Use of Force, the shooter must be able to identify the hands of the Threat/target. Leading with the eyes will allow for a momentary scan of the targets hands. Target discrimination skills will degrade quickly. Target discrimination drills should be a staple of training to identify: Threat, No Threat, Does not Currently Present a Threat.

Movement Package is an all-encompassing way of referencing multiple movements that will allow the shooter to obtain the required position to eliminate the threat. As Shooters we must remember that the need for speed is crucial.

The shooter must beat his adversary to the draw; this may require turning, facing, retreating or moving behind cover or into any of the alternate shooting platforms.

The shooter must use as much movement as required. The shooter must understand that as tactical distances increase the more cover can be used to allow for a stable shooting platform that may allow for safety and ensure accuracy.

The Movement Package must be the method that best allows the shooter to accurately engage the threat at the given distance.

Every shooter has their preferences, and nobody has the definitive choice in what the best position is. When it comes down to making a decision, the trained shooter must weigh multiple considerations when choosing the desired movement package that will allow for a safer platform, that will allow for accurate shots to be placed in the threat at various distances, lighting conditions and environmental considerations.

One Step Movements [Offline and Diagonal (Right and Left) and Forward/Back]

It should be noted that a proper understanding of a shooting platform may lend foot and/or body positioning in a more aggressive or even unbalanced position. The following steps are based upon a basic starting point for movement.

The step with the first foot is not so wide as to unbalance the shooter and the second step brings that along until both feet are under the shooter, shoulder width apart, for balance. The foot is lifted and placed down without dragging for the second step.
At the end of the movement, the feet should be under the body. A short, balanced movement finished in a balanced position provides a controlled platform for the shot. Both feet are lifted during the step, NO DRAG STEP

Responsible Citizens Seeking Responsible Training

Head down. Weight should be over both feet, centered under the hips. Toes should point at the threat.

Smooth movements let the shooter maintain balance for additional movements.

Do not hop or lunge. This will disturb the weapon's presentation, destroy the shooter's balance, cause unnecessary weapon movement and over balance the movement, making it difficult to move again.

The individual movements are as follows:

Offline Right or Left - The direction (right or left) the shooter intends to move is led by the foot on that side, Right, by the right and Left, by the left. Do not cross over with a step.

Forward or Back – Small, heel-to-toe steps (forward) or toe-to-heel steps (back). The beginning foot does not matter.

Responsible Citizens Seeking Responsible Training

Diagonal - From the start position the shooter will step either forward or rearward, at a 45-degree angle from the centerline. The shooter will step with the foot that is on the side he or she is moving toward first. Right Front Diagonal, right foot lead. Left Rear Diagonal, left foot lead

Continuous Offline Movement
The combining of any number of left, right, forward, and rear steps to provide a moving target for adversaries.

Hips are slightly dropped, moving by pulling with the front foot (rather than pushing with the rear) creating a gliding motion.

Continuous Forward Movement (Fighting toward your adversary)
Again, the below steps are optimum for shooters that have been walking almost their entire lives. A proper platform ensures that the shooter stays on target while performing a task that is certainly second nature.

The shooter's upper body stays weight forward, head down behind the weapon.
Taking small heel-to-toe steps with their toes pointing at the target, the shooter glides forward, maintaining their upper body level.

The legs act as shock absorbers, smoothing out any bounce in the step.

A smooth movement that maintains shooter control is the goal.

It should always be noted that shooters should only move as fast as they can accurately hit the target. As the shooter starts from a greater distance, single more accurate shots should be utilized. As the distance decreases and the target becomes closer, controlled pairs or a failure drill may be utilized.

The object is to continue to move while engaging the target. The shooter should not stop to fire. As the distance

Responsible Citizens Seeking Responsible Training

from the target increases, the slower the shot rhythm, as the distance decreases the faster the shot rhythm.

When moving forward, the shooter should move smoothly, taking small, evenly spaced steps to avoid unnecessary weapon movement. Move no faster than the body can be controlled or you can shoot accurately.

While moving forward, the heel contacts the ground first and the foot is rolled onto the toe.

The body should stay in a good shooting platform or "Fight" position. Special attention should be paid when backing, as the body has a tendency to raise itself upward.

The feet stay under the body and shoulder width apart. Do not cross the feet and legs when moving.

Move one step, left or right, to perform reloads or malfunction procedures (don't stand still because it is more difficult to hit a moving target.)

Continuous Rearward Movement (Fight Out)

The shooter will take short steps, toe-to-heel with the foot placement.
The upper body will stay as still as possible to eliminate bounce or sway.
The shooter's head will stay down behind the weapon.
Smooth movement is the goal, not speed.

While backing away, the toe contacts the ground first and the foot is rolled back onto the heel. Do not drag the feet. Dragging the feet can cause the shooter to trip or identify their position by noise.

Move one step, left or right, to perform reloads or malfunction procedures (Don't Stand Still)

Responsible Citizens Seeking Responsible Training

Lateral Movement
When moving to the left or right, the lower body behaves as in the forward technique. However, the upper body is twisted at the hips in order to present the weapon to the threat. This ensures optimum recoil management during movement.

When moving in the direction that is opposite to the shooter's strong hand, the shooter may have difficulty in smoothly presenting the weapon. The left-handed shooter may place the handgun in the strong hand only when moving to the right or use the backward moving technique with both hands. If the responsible citizen is outgunned or if the situation requires that getting to cover is paramount, the shooter should move with the utmost speed to a position of cover. If cover is the life-saving issue, then run, don't shoot.

90 Degree Pivots (Right and Left)
In all pivot movements, the shooter's head must turn first. This leads the body into the movement and identifies the target to set up the initial visual target line. The weapon must also remain in the holster until the shooter is facing the target. This will eliminate the shooter sweeping the firing line

The shooter's initial or start point is facing left or right at 90 degrees to the target line. On command, the shooter quickly snaps the head in the direction of the command; looks at the threat and identifies the target to be engaged. There are three primary ways to pivot to the threat:

Using a facing movement (Right face, Left face, etc.) by pivoting on the primary direction heel (right pivot, right heel) and remaining toe (right pivot, left foot toe), the shooter pivots into the threat direction and simply performs a "One Step Forward" as the weapon is presented.

The shooter pivots into the target, stepping toward the threat. The foot away from the target steps around in a half circle while the foot nearest the threat pivots. As the shooter presents their frontal area to the target, the weapon is presented to the target as the shooter faces the threat.

Pivoting away from the threat (startle response as shooter moves away from threat and hands move up to block potential blows), the shooter takes a half step back as the weapon is presented to the threat.

Responsible Citizens Seeking Responsible Training

180 Degree Pivots (Right and Left)

The shooter's initial or start point is facing away from the target. The shooter turns his head, looking over the designated shoulder and identifies the target to be engaged.

The shooter pivots to the target, stepping towards or away from the threat (as described above) as the shooter faces the target, the weapon is presented directly to the target.

Responsible Citizens Seeking Responsible Training

Responsible Citizens Seeking Responsible Training

Environmental Package

Responsible Citizens Seeking Responsible Training

Environmental Package is an all-encompassing way of referencing a multiple ENVIROMENTAL FACTORS that will allow the shooter to obtain the required position to eliminate the threat.

As Shooters, we must remember that the need for speed is crucial. The shooter must beat his adversary to the draw, this may require turning, facing, retreating or moving behind cover or into any of the alternate shooting platforms.

The shooter must use as much movement required.

The shooter must understand that as the threat distance increases the more cover can be used to allow for a stable shooting platform that may allow for safety and ensure accuracy.

The Movement Package must be the method that best allows the shooter to accurately engage the threat at the given distance with any shooting position that is presented.

Every shooter has their preferences, and nobody has the definitive choice in what the best position is. When it comes down to making a decision, the trained shooter must weigh multiple considerations. The optimal movement package should allow the shooter to create a safer platform that will allow for accurate shots at various distances, lighting conditions, and environmental considerations.

Breathing
Breath control is important to the aiming process of shooting because movement is required. If the shooter breathes while trying to aim, the rise and fall of his chest causes the weapon to move vertically. The shooter must

continue breathing during sight alignment, but he should hold a breath to complete the process of aiming.

A respiratory cycle lasts 4 to 5 seconds. Inhalation and exhalation requires only about 2 seconds. Thus, between each respiratory cycle, a pause of 2 to 3 seconds occurs. The pause can be expanded to 12 to 15 seconds without any special effort or unpleasant sensation; however, the maximum safe pause is 8 to 10 seconds.

Barricades
Firing from a barricaded position is an essential part of combat marksmanship. It is a relatively straightforward skill, and easily acquired. As all shooting techniques, however, mastery only comes from extensive practice Common sense dictates that when being shot at, the reasonable person will try to find cover from incoming rounds. If withdrawal from the scene is not practical and returning fire is justified, then knowledge of barricade position firing is essential.

The most important part of the barricaded position is being behind the barricade.

The only portions of your body that should be exposed beyond the barricade are your firing hand and only the

Responsible Citizens Seeking Responsible Training

amount of your face that is needed to obtain a clear view of the sights, target, and situation. While the shooter is up against the barricade, it's also very easy to place the side of the firearm against the side of the barricade in an effort to better stabilize it. This technique may cause the exact opposite effect on your accuracy. When your firearm goes off, the recoil will force the side of your firearm to bounce off the side of the barricade causing the barrel of the firearm to move off target resulting in an inaccurate shot. It should be noted that in most circumstances, the further "back" from cover the shooter is positioned, the less the shooter may be exposed to direct or flanking fire (shooting against elevated positions and very low barricades withstanding).

One Handed Shooting Techniques

When shooting, every shooter should attempt to perform at a level where there is a proper Balance of Speed and Accuracy (BSA). When shooting the handgun, speed will not come automatically; it comes only after repeatedly practicing the basic skill sets. Speed is important, but not at the expense of accuracy. A slow hit will beat a fast miss every time. Each responsible citizen should push themselves to their limit as long as the basics are not neglected. Consistency in all techniques is a key element to attaining BSA, always performing the techniques or procedure the same way.

Strong Hand Only
The stance must generally become more aggressive. The grip is the key to shooting well one-handed. Grip the weapon as high possible without affecting the function of the weapons system. The thumb is the true key to effective one-handed shooting.

The thumb may be positioned in one of two ways for effective shooting.

The thumb may be forced down on to the middle finger. This technique requires the shooter to rotate the thumb down until it touches the middle finger with some amount of force.

The most effective technique for most shooters is the high thumb. It is advantageous to have the thumb pointing up to ensure the wrist tendon is locked and helping support the push back of the weapon.

Support Hand Only (Other Strong Hand)

The support hand grips are identical to the Strong hand only grip. When shooting with the support hand only, the shooter must modify the position of the sight package in one of two ways. Use the support side eye or push the weapon further to the strong side to use the dominate eye. I have found that once a shooter really starts to enter the arena of "advanced shooting" that support hand is a must. This will trigger the brain to notice all the small imperfections that have developed with your strong side shooting techniques.

One Handed Shooting Survival Techniques.
The ability to solve weapon problems during an active altercation/gunfight with one hand increases the survivability. As long as the mind is working and having

the use of at least one hand, the shooter can still defend one-self with a handgun. Handgrip is the key ingredient for shooting well with one hand.

Any problem that can be solved using two hands should also be solvable with one hand. Strong hand or support hand only. The draw, reloads, malfunctions and manipulations.

The grip must be established as high as possible without affecting the function of the weapon. Ensure the web of the hand is placed as high as possible on the back strap of the pistol. A poor grip may induce malfunctions. Two options for a one hand grip are:

A thumbs high grip allows for the tendon in the shooting hand to be locked. This will provide additional leverage and can be advantageous in managing recoil.

Thumb to middle finger is the opposite of the high thumb grip. This technique requires the shooter to rotate the shooting thumb down until it is pressed against the middle finger. By pressing down and not just resting the shooting thumb on the middle finger the shooter may lock the shooting wrist tendon.

Draw and Presentation. Drawing with strong hand - The weapon is drawn in the same normal manner out of the holster. Drawing with the support hand. Reach across with the support hand and unsnap the holster. Raise the weapon only enough to clear the trigger guard and turn the weapon around in the holster until the butt/magazine floor plate faces forward. Using the holster for support, establish a grip, draw the weapon and present the weapon toward the threat.

An alternate method is to "trap" the weapon against the belly and roll the grip into the support hand to firmly establish control of the weapon.

Strong and Support Hand Emergency reloads--
Reloading with the slide locked to the rear.

When the weapon is held in one hand, the magazine release button is depressed by the following action: right hand - use thumb; left hand - use index finger. The weapon is secured either between the thighs or in the bend behind the knees

Responsible Citizens Seeking Responsible Training

(for static/behind cover) or in the holster or waistband with the magazine well exposed (for movement). The operable hand retrieves a magazine from the pouch. Using the operable hand, the fully prepared magazine is inserted into the magazine well.

Establish a firm grip on the weapon with the operable hand; ensure that the trigger finger is outside the trigger guard. Once the muzzle is pointed in the direction of their threat, release the slide by one of the methods described below. Any of these procedures will chamber a round.

Release the slide by depressing the slide catch with either the right-hand thumb or left-hand index finger. Release the slide by hooking the rear sight against a hard object such as the gun belt, holster, heel of a boot/shoe, and the edge of a wall or a desktop. Push down with the weapon so that the slide is pushed back and the slide catch is released. Shooters must be cautious not to allow an object to interfere with the slide going forward or a failure to feed malfunction may occur.

Allow the slide to go forward freely. DO NOT RIDE THE SLIDE FORWARD!! Visually check the weapon to verify the slide locked into battery.

One Handed Survival Techniques Primary Malfunction Procedures (Tap-Rack-Ready)
Take the finger off the trigger and place it alongside the frame. TAP the bottom of the magazine against the thigh on the side where the weapon is located or on another firm object to ensure that the magazine is seated properly.

RACK the slide by hooking the rear sight against a hard object such as the gun belt, holster, and heel of a boot/shoe, edge of a wall or a desktop. Push down with the weapon so that the slide is pushed back and the slide catch is released. Shooters must be cautious not to allow an object to interfere with the slide going forward or a failure to feed malfunction may occur.

Responsible Citizens Seeking Responsible Training

READY is when the weapon is removed from the secured area with the operable hand and now is ready to resume threat engagement or active threat cover measures.

One Handed Survival Techniques Secondary Malfunctions (Rip-Work Reload Ready)
Push on the magazine release button and hook the lip of the magazine floor plate on the gun belt, holster or other firm object that will offer some resistance and push weapon away from the hooked floor plate to RIP it from the well

WORK the slide two or three times by hooking the rear sight against a hard object such as a gun belt, holster, heel of a boot/shoe, the edge of a wall, or a desktop.

Temporarily holster or secure the weapon to insert a new magazine. Re-draw the weapon then TAP the bottom of the magazine against thigh or another firm object to ensure that the magazine is seated properly
RACK the slide by hooking the rear sight against a hard surface or using the slide stop lever.

Extreme Close Quarters Position. One Hand. This position is attained when the pistol is being drawn but the threat is too close to extend out due to the possibility of the adversary reaching and grabbing the weapon. Shooter maintains an aggressive shooting platform throughout entire draw and presentation. The draw stroke stops when the pistol is at the apex (basically stopping a normal draw stroke). The weapon is held one handed, strong hand only, slightly canted away from the body, magazine floor plate resting against the rib cage.

The support hand grips the back of your own neck with the bicep pressed against the head and the forearm pressed against the temple in a high blocking or striking position. In an actual confrontation, the support hand may also be defensively engaged.

Depending on the situation, the weapon muzzle should be directed either center mass of the threat, or toward the lower torso of the threat (lower abdomen or pelvic region). For center mass shots, ensure the support hand is behind or on top of the head to mitigate the potential for self-inflicted wounds of the support arm. Minimize blading of the body while remaining weight forward.

Combatants will often have their hands occupied during encounters. Students should practice clearing their hands of unnecessary objects (i.e. notepads, coffee cups, etc.) when reacting to an immediate threat.

Objects can be dropped or thrown toward the threat as a diversion.

Two Hand. This position is used when the pistol is held in the high compression position (modified position 3) and the threat is too close to extend out and to keep mechanical advantage (of the pistol) away from the threat. The high compression platform reduces shoulder tension (over a normal two-hand close quarters position), makes grip retention easier, and brings the weapon into the sight line without creating shoulder/arm tension.

From a normal close quarters/ready position (or position 3), the strong wrist is pronated with the index or reference point being the top edge of the weapon slide held vertical along the body's centerline. The weapon is rolled inboard (magazine well facing out).
A normal two-handed grip may give mechanical advantage to an adversary in extreme close quarters. From the high compression platform, the two-handed retention position enables the weapon to be used in prying to disengage, striking, or conducting a contact shot. From the high compression platform, the support hand thumb, index, and middle finger move forward (on the slide) and form a "C" clamp just forward of the trigger guard, clamping down hard on the slide. This position reduces the possibility of weapon take away. As the contact shot is fired, the friction created by the support hand grip (on the slide) causes the slide NOT to cycle. As the shooter creates distance, the support hand moves to the grasping grooves and cycles the slide, ejecting the spent casing and loading another round ("…rack/ready or reassess". The "tap" being unnecessary).

Responsible Citizens Seeking Responsible Training

Standing (Close Quarters Distance) – Feet shoulder width apart, firing foot slightly back. Toes facing threat area, shoulders square to your threat (DO NOT BLADE). Establish a slightly exaggerated squat, weight on the balls of feet, aggressive and forward. Body should not move, only the weapon should move.

Responsible Citizens Seeking Responsible Training

Seated (in a chair or seat) - The shooter should be balanced in the seat. As the threat is recognized, the legs are pulled underneath the seat to facilitate ease of movement (standing and/or pivoting). At the same time the legs are moving, the shooter performs a quick area scan before drawing the weapon. The weapon is presented to the threat as safely as possible and the requisite number of rounds are fired. As the threat is neutralized, the shooter returns the weapon to close quarters/position 3/high compression platform, performs another area scan to include directly behind, and decides whether movement is required, standing to safely re-holster

Responsible Citizens Seeking Responsible Training

Responsible Citizens Seeking Responsible Training

Seated Pivots (in a chair or seat)

Responsible Citizens Seeking Responsible Training

Kneeling (Increased Mobility) – Establish same upper-torso shooting platform from firing one knee down. When shooting from a distance, lower the center of gravity by sitting on firing knee and resting at least one elbow on support knee (Soft tissue to soft tissue or bone to soft tissue, never bone to bone. High Kneeling: Shooter's may drop to both knees simultaneously or down to one knee (decreased mobility) Low Kneeling: Strong side ankle is turned with the outside of the foot in contact with the ground or toes down in contact with the ground. Buttocks are either in contact with the inside of the strong foot or seated on the heel. Shooter's weight is on the back side of the strong leg. Of the kneeling positions, the low kneeling position offers the greatest stability, but further limits mobility.

Responsible Citizens Seeking Responsible Training

High Kneeling: Shooter's may drop to both knees simultaneously or down to one knee (decreased mobility)

Low Kneeling: Strong side ankle is turned with the outside of the foot in contact with the ground or toes down in contact with the ground. Buttocks are either in contact with the inside of the strong foot or seated on the heel. Shooter's weight is on the back side of the strong leg. Of the kneeling positions, the low kneeling position offers the greatest stability, but further limits mobility.

Low/Rice Paddy Squat – From standing position, squat as low as possible with feet spread wide. Both feet must be in total contact with the ground to prevent rocking. If done correctly, it is a very stable and highly mobile position.

As responsible citizens we must understand and be able to discuss the pros and cons of multiple techniques. We must understand that the technique is a way to accomplish the task at hand, not THE way. Each shooter will have to determine what works best for them. It is also imperative that a shooter understands that just because the instructor cannot accomplish the assigned task with the technique chosen, does not mean that the student cannot use that technique to accomplish the task.

Do not confuse competition with combat. Certain competition skills and styles may or may not have a place in the combat/tactical world. An instructor should be familiar with these techniques so that the discussion of pros, cons, whys and why not's may be had.
As responsible citizens we must not forget why we are training and what we are planning to accomplish. We are training to stop a threat to ourselves and our loved ones and this cannot be taken lightly. We are planning to win, not just survive.

Bi-lateral Shooting
A right or left-handed shooter up against the barricade may need to shoot on the opposite side of the barricade. Transfer your firearm into your opposite hand. This may complicate and slow down the ability to place continuous accurate shots on an assailant unless proper bi-lateral training is conducted. The idea or premise behind switching gun hands from one or the other is that an individual will expose less of his or her body when peeking out from behind the side of an obstacle like the corner of a wall. The shooter must ensure that the thumbs of both the "new" strong hand and "new" support hand are on the same side of the pistol and that proper eye dominance is maintained.

Alternate Positions- In order to be a responsible citizen you must have the ability to provide quick and accurate fire, no matter the position. Know what your body can do.

All advanced tactical platforms are based upon what is naturally going to happen under stress. Static movements

Responsible Citizens Seeking Responsible Training

evolve into natural movements. Efficiency equals economy of motion AND effort. Speed is a byproduct of efficiency.

Low Light Fundamentals. A majority of shootings and confrontations happen in low light conditions. You cannot fight what you cannot see, nor can your opponent. Do not shoot at muzzle flash or silhouettes only. A responsible citizen should always identify the target! You should not engage what you don't know. Bottom line: the pressure of time, the activation of your powerful sympathetic nervous system and the compelling desire to prevail can easily lead to a misidentification of an individual

As a responsible citizen, if you keep a gun in your house keep a flashlight next to it. . A responsible citizen should always identify the target

Why use light? Control. The hot spot directed in suspects eyes. Use light to control and direct movements and restrict the attacker's visual data.

For a communication tool – Use the flashlight as a pointer.
.
Power with Light. From: Clearly viewing the world without interruption and without error. To: Seeing nothing but brilliant white light(s) and no clear comprehension of force deployment.

Placing the "hot spot", the most intense part of the light beam directly into the suspect's eyes. You are flooding the "correct space" with photons. When supporting this principal, you are creating a temporary "white wall of light" that allows you a greater variety of deployment options.

Power with light, broken up with Light and move. Threats not isolated…Light and Move option.

Disorient by Oscillation/Strobing. The effect of rapid oscillation and/or strobing lights will alter the suspect's spatial orientation and depth perception. Best used during the "Light and Move" technique. The light becomes the "jab", the gun the "cross".

Align three things. Eyes, weapon and light should be aligned as much as the situation allows. No matter the technique used, the hot spot should be where it should be. Do not stare at the sights, they should be in battery, hinged just below the finial sight plane, ready to be reattached to the vision if the need to reengage arises.

OODA Cycle Applied in Low Light.

OBSERVE. Attempt to find your opponent first (create a false picture or illusion with your light). Once threats are located, attempt to unbalance by "10-ringing" threats with large quantities of light, stopping threats from processing useful data freely.

ORIENT. Identify the layout and hazards in the area. If a human target appears, identify as a shoot or no-shoot. Disorient by attacking the opponents "Radar system" with random fluctuations or overwhelm it with energy.

DECIDE. Incoming data is immediately parsed into one of two pathways; Conscious – sequential, deliberate, and variables limited. Sub-conscious – parallel, distributed network, and time-efficient

ACT. All action should be preceded by 3 phases: Observation, Orientation, and Decision. A reasonable amount of training should be in context of mission specific

Responsible Citizens Seeking Responsible Training

requirements. Introduce the correct type of stress in training to produce proper actions when required

Low light and Flashlight Techniques.
The ability to perform efficient weapons handling skills should transfer into all lighting conditions. Kinesthetic ability and training should render these procedures into reflexive behavior. It is not merely desirable to become proficient at shooting with the aid of a flashlight, it should be a critical part of the tactical skillset and not be relegated to a one-time event. Being skilled and comfortable at simultaneously operating a firearm and flashlight enables a responsible citizen to focus on safely performing the job at hand, rather than becoming distracted by equipment issues and/or dangerous tactical errors

Maintain the proper mindset – confident, controlling, and dominating any actual or potential threat

Additional Information

Responsible Citizens Seeking Responsible Training

Instructor methods

The goal of my training philosophies and concepts are designed to challenge firearms instructors to take a critical look at traditional philosophies and methodologies.

These concepts equips firearms instructors with the knowledge and techniques required to reinforce the fundamentals of tactical shooting and weapons handling skills that will be encountered under stress.

This information is designed to enhance knowledge and educate firearms instructors so that they can teach the principles of advanced tactical shooting and move their training programs to the next level by emphasizing the concept of gun fighting principals and using specific techniques such as the thumbs forward grip, proper body bio-mechanics, committed shot trigger control, and movement (all of which are designed to enhance the shooter's weapon control and ability to engage multiple targets), this will allow you to dominate the weapon and situation.

A firearms instructor should be able to demonstrate that the basics can be performed to perfection on demand and have their students validate the principle taught.

Drills must support the skill being taught.
Shooting drills that have standards allow shooters to track performance over time.

A structured training program with performance tracking is the difference between training and "plinking."

The key is to identify the drills that are relevant to your end goals and your current skill level.

Instructors are much better off running drills that focus on accuracy and fundamentals with speed gradually added.

Spend the majority of your time working on the skills that you're most likely to need.

Once shooter feel that they can shoot relatively fast, tighten up the scoring zone or increase the distance.

Push shooters past their comfort zones.

Once shooters surpass their previous comfort zones, back them down with the need for increased accuracy.
Instructors that do not push speed are setting their students up for failure.

Speed equals pressure, which equals learning or failure.

Targets
When selecting a training target, the instructor needs to consider what the lesson is being taught. When selecting a training target, the instructor needs to consider if the target supports the drill understand the Pros of the selected target. Understand the Cons of the selected Target. Targets come in all shapes and sizes for their intended training purpose. Steel Targets provide instant feedback. Paper Targets provide a measurable record. Negative targets (removing the scoring ring to create a hole) will increase the speed of the student by removing visual stimulus. Each style will guide your goals as an instructor and shooter to enhance the range sessions

Paper Shooting Targets – Paper targets help shooters sight-in advanced rifles and are commonly used for law enforcement agency qualifications. Paper targets allow people to precisely see where their shots hit, which is important for illustrating group shots, where shooters are supposed to hit the target in the same place each time. Paper targets come in a wide variety of shapes and sizes, including offering score zones, qualification criteria for matches and different shooting stages. Paper targets are more affordable and flexible for some shooting events.

Bull's-eye targets. Some people don't think you can learn to fire in combat effectively by practicing bull's eye marksmanship. Firmly in the bullseye camp are the United States Marines, who teach marksmanship on known-distance ranges with round-bull's-eye targets. Last time we checked, no one wanted to stand in front of a bunch of Marines and taunt them about their marksmanship.

Human-shaped targets. The military and police generally teach a center-of-mass shot, but count any hit on the paper or on the silhouette as a hit. In an actual firefight, only disabling rounds count, and the area is much narrower and smaller than a classic GI E-type silhouette. (In this, the classic FBI target with its higher-scoring vital area is superior). It's hard to aim for the center of a silhouette unless you've had a lot of practice. In particular, shooters at the same level of experience have a lot more vertical dispersion on silhouettes than they do on a round bull's-eye. Silhouette Paper target- it should have an easily scoreable area to allow for penalizing the shooter who isn't quite as accurate.

Steel. When a shooter fires at steel targets, typically he/she is met with both visual and auditory replies. Steel targets offer immediate feedback, as the shooter can tell through visual confirmation if the target is hit. The shooter can hear if the bullet meets the steel, making his/her time on the shooting range even more productive. Metal targets that reset, known as jumping targets, allow shooters to spend more time on the range instead of reconfiguring targets.

Types of Paper Targets

IDPA Competition Target

PSC/USPSA CARDBOARD TORSO TARGET

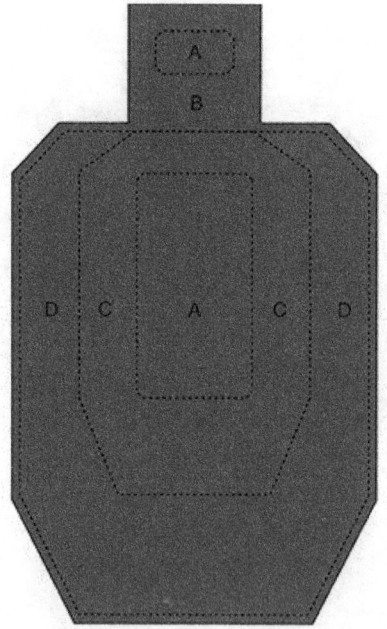

B-8 Bullseye Target

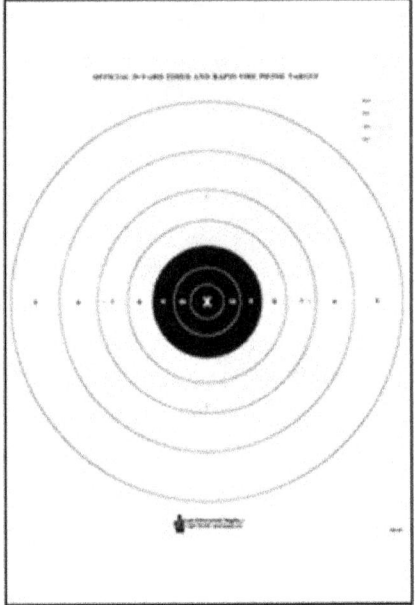

Responsible Citizens Seeking Responsible Training

US MARSHALS SERVICE QUALIFICATION TARGET

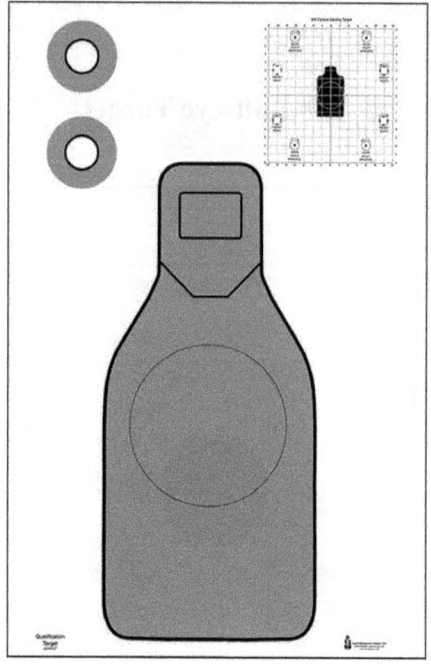

FLETC ADVANCED TRAINING TARGET

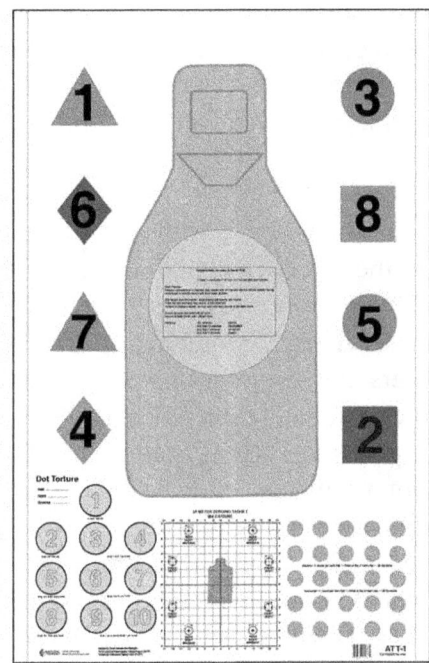

Responsible Citizens Seeking Responsible Training

Skills Assessments - Course of Fire
Skills Assessments and Courses of Fire are nothing more than a series of drill running in a continuous fashion. Use PSA and CoFs to establish baseline competency and track improvement over time. PSA and CoFs should provide a measurable standard that you can track over time.

Tips for the Trainer
Before the first round is fired, you must make a commitment to the safety/range policy and this class. An unsafe person on the range will carry his habits into the field. If you observe one shooter acting unsafely, chances are other shooters are doing the same thing. Stop the drill and explain to everyone that unsafe acts will not be tolerated. It is your responsibility to correct deficiencies. An unsafe shooter will kill or injure another shooter. An example of an unsafe shooter would be a shooter who keeps his finger on the trigger at all times. Stop him the very first time he does this and train him to place his firing finger outside the trigger guard until he has actually committed himself to engage a target.

Dry firing (firing with an unloaded weapon) develops and improves every element of shooting. Dry firing improves the shooter's ability to align his sights properly. It minimizes his arc of movement. It also develops precise and uniformly coordinated trigger control. Every marksmanship session should begin with 10 to 15 minutes of dry fire. In an era of less ammunition, dry fire is invaluable. No range is needed, and the equipment is organic. STRESS DRY FIRE!

Begin the marksmanship training with slow aimed fire, this allows the shooter to concentrate on the fundamentals. Also, if you are trying to identify shooters with shooting problems, it will be easier to identify what the shooter is doing wrong, because most new shooters violate several fundamentals at the same time.

Front load all the double-action shooting into the first few sessions. Double-action shooting requires more training than single-action shooting. More time is needed to train trigger control and develop muscle memory when taking up trigger slack.

Focusing on the front sight is the most important fundamental prior to the shot breaking. Shooters will usually focus on the target; they want to sneak a peek at where the round hit. The eye can focus at only one distance at a time; that focus should be on the front sight. An excellent way to train shooters to focus on the front sight is to dot the front sight with typewriter white out. Blackout the rear sight. The white dot against an all-black background should catch the attention of the shooter, and it is easier to concentrate on.

If you have a shooter who cannot keep pace with the session, pull him out and give him one on one instruction. Start with some ball and dummy drills. This will determine if he is jerking the trigger. It will also make his mistake more evident to the shooter. Place him on the 3 meter line if necessary to build up his self-confidence. Thirty minutes of personalized instruction will accomplish more for the shooter than four hours of training in which he is overwhelmed.

The shooting program must be flexible enough to change and progress according to the abilities of the shooters. If everyone is doing well at 10 meters, challenge them, move them back to 15 meters. This will require more concentration. If everyone is having trouble shooting at 10 meters, move them in closer to reinforce the fundamentals.

When a new exercise or technique is taught, shot groups will usually widen, because the students are concentrating on the new drill rather than the basics. Tell them to start off slow and concentrate on the basics. Remember, slow is smooth and smooth is fast. Don't forget to start the new exercise with dry fire.

The last exercise of the day should be one that everyone can do well. This ensures the shooters will have confidence in themselves for the next day's session. This will hold true especially for shooters having a bad day or those that feel they will never be able to shoot.
Weapons cleaning should also incorporate inspecting the weapon.

Shooting 3-inch dots requires more concentration than shooting 25-yard bull's-eyes at short distances. When a shooter has a larger target area, the tendency is to shoot a wider dispersion pattern. As proficiency increases, you should require more from the shooter. Use smaller targets or greater distances. A small white pasties in the center of a bull's-eye will give the shooter a more distinct target and may decrease the size of his shot groups.
When engaging multiple targets, most shooters will not remove the weapon from their face. They will get target fixation and move directly toward the targets, unaware of their surroundings. This is a dangerous habit that needs to be broken. A weapon in the face obscures low targets and furniture on the floor. Stress the importance of dropping the barrel of the weapon 3 to 4 inches after the target has been engaged. This will allow the shooter to take a quick look at the area.

Man-on-man competition is one of the most effective methods of accelerating shooter development. Midway through the program incorporate some competitive shooting. Make sure all shooters participate in the match. This will induce the shooters to push their abilities and see where other shooters have developed.

In later sessions incorporate whistle drills. When shooting most drills, the individual will fire when he is ready. Use the whistle as the stimulus for the shooters. This forces the shooter to react more quickly. Like competition, whistle drills will accelerate shooter development.

After the shooters have been introduced to magazine changes, it is a good idea to have the shooters fill each other's magazines'. In this way no individual will know exactly how many rounds are in the magazine; therefore, he will not be able to predict when the weapon will run dry.

It may not be advisable to conduct shooting and moving drills in wet weather. If the soil retains a lot of moisture, the shooters might slip while moving with a loaded weapon. Anytime a shooting and moving drill is being conducted, the shooters should wear all their individual equipment, to include body armor. This will begin enforcing the skills necessary and develop muscle memory.

A range box should be kept on each range. The box should contain hammers, different sized nails, several staplers, staples, pasties, tape, and different types of targets, spray paint, garbage bags, cleaning equipment, and counseling forms. Inspect the box after each range session, and you will not be caught short the next day.

Responsible Citizens Seeking Responsible Training

From the Team Room Wall

Things to remember

*Accuracy takes precedence over speed. "The most important thing is to hit what you are shooting at. No matter what else happens, you must hit your target."

*Learn to apply your skills on demand. "Consistent top performers in any sport have a thorough understanding of the basics and have learned to apply the principles at all times. Don't be distracted from the shooting."

*You must compete at your natural body speed. "Don't attempt to speed up or slow down. You must learn to allow it to happen."

*Speed is economy of motion. "Every move is directed toward gaining something. There is no wasted motion or effort."

*Speed will increase through practice; it is a byproduct of proper training and technique. "You don't have to try to be fast. As your skill increases and you are able to execute at the subconscious level, speed increases naturally."

*Let the sights dictate your cadence of fire. "Sight alignment is your speedometer–it shows you how fast you can or cannot go. If the sights are acceptably aligned, fire the shot. If the sights are not acceptably aligned, don't fire the shot until they are–whether it takes a quarter-second, half-second or two seconds."

*Learn what an acceptable sight picture is, and trigger squeeze for the required shot. "Quality of sight alignment for a 15-yard shot is not as exact as for a 50-yard shot. You'd like to always see perfect sight alignment, but you must learn to accept less if it will still allow you to hit your target."

*Shoot one shot at a time. The next shot you are about to fire is the most important one of your life. "Don't fall into the trap of thinking of strings of fire. A match [or a fight] is won shooting one shot at a time."

*When all else fails, align the sights and squeeze the prepped trigger. No matter what else happens, if you align the sights and squeeze the prepped trigger, you will hit the target."

Most importantly: there is no such thing as an advanced gunfight…just gunfights in which the fundamentals were performed to near perfection on demand."

Responsible Citizens Seeking Responsible Training

Favorite Shooting Drills

Understand what skills that the shooter is desiring to test. What tasks or techniques will support the testing of this skill? Multiple skills will also be used to map out a course of fire.

When I teach a class, I tell my students that there are only two drills that count. The first one of the day and the last one.

The first drill of the day is designed to be shot cold, so no warm up! This will give you a reading on your true skills. There is no warm up in a gun fight.

Shoot the drill cold with your carry gun, in a holster the way you carry daily and with the ammunition you carry daily in the gun.

Pick a drill that allows for you to set a measurable standard.

Shoot the drill at the start of all your range sessions.

My preferred drill as mentioned in the beginning is the **Ken Hackathorn Wizard Drill.** It is quick (5 rounds) and lets you know if you are competent enough to carry a gun!

If time is of the essence, I will shoot a 25meter bullseye. Whenever I am teaching in New Hampshire, regardless of time of year; I get off the plane and head to the Sig Sauer Academy grab some rounds and head back to the 25 meter pistol range. With the pistol I carried up with me, I shoot a 25 yard bullseye for score! This allows me a benchmark to see how well I am doing on any given day!

Pick a drill that works for you. Have a standard and keep track of your ability!

Shot on 14 December 2017 at the Sig Sauer Academy 25 Meter Bullseye in the snow. 23 degrees!

If time permits, I try to finish up a class with **the 700 Point Aggregate "The Humbler"**

The last drill allows for you to test yourself when you are tired and ready to be finished. It will make you dig down deep into your soul to see what you are made of!

The drill uses NRA B-8 bullseye targets at a range of 25 yards. A fresh target is used for each string to minimize scoring errors. *Rounds impacting outside the marked scoring zones are zero points.*

Responsible Citizens Seeking Responsible Training

The Wizard Drill that was designed by Ken Hackathrorn as a basic competency evaluation for carrying a pistol for personal defense. I had the privilege of spending the day with Ken in Florida and from this instructors view he lived up to the "Yoda" moniker. It was a true pleasure to state what ideas and concepts that I practiced and believed in and then receive confirmation that I was spot on from him. This was a watershed instructor moment for me. It is always good to receive affirmation on your beliefs from a legend. I did come to the realization that the only score that counts is the first one of the day, shot cold! After that the training begins.

I use the Wizard Drill as an entrance exam when I teach an intermediate or advanced class. The drill only takes 5 rounds and can be conducted rather quickly. This drill is designed to test the shooter with the equipment and ammo that you carry and to be shot cold.

Each string in this drill must be fired in 2 ½ seconds or less. The drill requires only 5 rounds. This drill will allow the shooter to measure their ability to balance speed and accuracy since and accurate shot must be place in a required time!

The evaluation was designed to be shot on an IPSC type target with a head and body box.

Stage 1) 3 yard line, one hand shooting one shot to the head
Stage 2) 5 yard line, two handed shooting, one shot to the head
Stage 3) 7 yard line, two handed shooting, one shot to the head
Stage 4) 10 yard line, two handed shooting, two shots to the body

At the completion of the evaluation the shooter should have fired each stage in 2 ½ seconds or less. Each stage starts with the gun in the holster. The shooter should have 3 shots in the head box and 2 shots in the body box.

The difficulty level can be increased by the target used. When using an ISPC type target the "A" zones are the target boxes.

When using a Sig "Brett" or "Doug" Target, the 4 inch face circle and 8 inch body circle are the scoring zones. Another variation to increase difficulty is doubling the round count and keeping the same time standards.

In a pinch and 3x5 card and a 5x8 card spray-glued on a target will work!

Remember, the drill is designed to be shot cold! This drill will let the shooter know their proficiency level and often humbles those that do not train as hard as they think they do. This is your benchmark!

700 Point Aggregate "The Humbler"

Stage 1: Slow Fire
    10 rounds
    Freestyle
    Time limit: ten minutes

Stage 2: Timed Fire from the holster
    5 rounds
    Freestyle from the holster time limit: 20 seconds
    Repeat a second time for total of 10 rounds fired

Stage 3: Rapid Fire from the holster
    5 rounds
    Freestyle from the holster
    Time limit: 10 seconds
    Repeat a second time for total of 10 rounds fired

Stage 4: SHO Slow Fire
    5 rounds
    Strong hand only
    Time limit: five minutes

Stage 5: SHO Timed Fire from the holster
    5 rounds
    Strong hand only from the holster
    Time limit: 20 seconds

Stage 6: SHO Rapid Fire from the holster
    5 rounds
    Strong hand only from the holster
    Time limit: 10 seconds

Stage 7: WHO Slow Fire
    5 rounds
    Support hand only
    Time limit: five minutes

Stage 8: Kneeling Slow Fire
    5 rounds
    Kneeling freestyle
    Time limit: five minutes

Stage 9: Kneeling Timed Fire from the holster
    5 rounds
    Begin standing, draw and kneel at buzzer
    Time limit: 20 seconds

Stage 10: Prone Slow Fire
    5 rounds
    Prone freestyle
    Time limit: five minutes

Stage 11: Prone Timed Fire from the holster
    5 rounds
    Begin standing, draw and go prone at buzzer
    Time limit: 20 seconds

The 700 Point Aggregate was designed as a total marksmanship test for SFOD-D at Fort Bragg North Carolina. It has been popularized by Larry Vickers. I was exposed to it by "Super" Dave Harrington while attending the US Army Special Forces Advanced Reconnaissance, Target Analysis and Exploitation Techniques Course (SFARTAETC).

A very challenging and time consuming course of fire!

300 Point Aggregate "The mini Humbler"

Stage 1: Slow Fire
- 10 rounds
- Freestyle
- Time limit: ten minutes

Stage 2: Timed Fire from the holster
- 5 rounds
- Freestyle from the holster time limit: 20 seconds
- *Repeat a second time for total of 10 rounds fired*

Stage 3: Rapid Fire from the holster
- 5 rounds
- Freestyle from the holster
- Time limit: 10 seconds
- *Repeat a second time for total of 10 rounds fired*

This version will allow you to shoot the 25 yard Marksmanship Bullseye.

The next Bullseye will add a little bit of timed fire and start to expose flaws

The finial Bullseye is the traditional speed bull

70%- 210
80%- 240
90%- 270

PISTOL STANDARDS-

These where designed by Paul Howe to be Instructor Standards. These are an excellent baseline and challenge for basic shooter. Start with being able to hit the target in time and as you get better the acceptable level of accuracy should get smaller.

The drills below drills are designed with three purposes in mind:
1. A measurable standard to maintain.
2. An efficient stair-stepped workout program that covers all the bases.
3. To test the individual shooter at various times to show areas needing improvement.

STANDARDS STANDARD
1. Ready 1 shot 1 target 7 yards **1 SEC**
2. Holster 1 shot 1 target 7 yards **1.7 SEC**
3. Ready 2 shots 1 target 7 yards **1.5 SEC**
4. Ready 5/1 shots 1 target 7 yards **3 SEC**
5. Ready 4 shots 2x target 7 yards **3 SEC**
6. Ready 4 shots 2x weak/2x strong (1target) **5 SEC**
7. Ready 1 shot Malfunction drill (1 target) **3 SEC**
8. Ready 4 shots 2 Reload 2 (1 target) **5 SEC**
9. Rifle up 1 shot Dry fire/transition **3.25**
10. Holster 1 shot kneeling (1 target) 25 yards **3.25**

Total: 25 Rounds
INSTRUCTORS MUST PASS 8-10 STANDARDS IN ONE COURSE OF FIRE.
-All stations shot at 7 yards except #10.

The F.A.S.T. Drill

Fundamentals, Accuracy, and Speed Test was designed by Todd Green. This evaluation is designed to be shot at 7 yards from the holster. I like this drill because it evaluates speed and accuracy together and adds the additional skill of an emergency reload. The drill was designed to be shot on a 3x5 card for the head and an 8 inch circle for the body. The shooter can download targets from various internet locations and print them out.

When using the Sig Academy "Brett" or "Doug" targets I use the 4 inch face circle and the 8 inch body circle and the same time standard. These targets or the US Marshal and FBI bowling pin targets or the FLETC ATT-1 work extremely well because the scoring boxes are farther apart than the conventional FAST downloaded targets.

Ranking

10+ seconds NOVICE
Less than 10 seconds INTERMEDIATE
Less than 7 seconds ADVANCED
Less than 5 seconds EXPERT

The shooter will load the pistol with a 2 round magazine and have a 4 round magazine for a reload. From the holster fire 2 to the head, emergency reload and fire 4 to the body.

The Devils Reload 6x6x6
This is a very demanding reload drill and one that I use as the finial evaluation when conducting reload training drills. The shooter will be warmed up since this is the last drill in a series. I got this one from my good friend "Super" Dave Harrington. The truth be told, SD was the NCOIC at Range 37 on Fort Bragg for my SOT and again for my SFARTEAC classes. SD truly enhanced my knowledge and put me on the road to shooting a pistol.

The drill is designed to be shot from the holster with three (3) six (6) round magazines. Draw and fire 6, emergency reload fire 6, emergency reload and fire the last 6. The drill is shot from the 7 yard line on a target with an 8 inch chest circle.

Ranking
15+ seconds NOVICE
13 seconds INTERMEDIATE
12 seconds ADVANCED
10 seconds EXPERT

This drill did help to remind me that there is always someone better than me. After breaking 10 seconds the first time I was pretty happy until SHOT show that year when I got to watch another friend, Max Michel shoot a version of 7x7x7 and he did it on 3 targets, so he added a target transition and he did it in 7 seconds!

Responsible Citizens Seeking Responsible Training

The Bill Drill
Designed by Bill Wilson as the story goes. This drill may be referred to as a "hammer drill" or rhythm drill.

This drill reinforces the draw stroke. Rapid fire and recoil management.

The drill was designed to be shot on an IPSC target from 7 yards. I will often use a Sig "Brett" or "Doug" or the US Marshal "Q" or the FLETC ATT-1. Any target with a designated hit zone.

The target will depend on your acceptable level of accuracy. I think an 8 inch circle at 7 yards will work!

The drill is designed to be shot from the holster, draw and fire six (6) rounds. If a shot misses the scoreable zone then it does not count.

Ranking
5 seconds NOVICE
4 seconds INTERMEDIATE
3 seconds ADVANCED
2 seconds EXPERT

Mozambique Drill

The drill is often just called two (2) to the body, one (1) to head as history becomes lost. I remember this one being discussed in *Soldier of Fortune* back in the early days.

The drill will work target acquisition, multiple targets (body and head) and multiple threats (two Targets) and a reload.

This drill can be shot on any target that has a distinct separation of head and body. If a challenge is required a 3x5 card and a 5x8 card spray glued on a plain background will work.

Prep two (2) magazines with three (3) rounds each. From the draw, fire two (2) rounds to the body, transition your eyes to the head and then move your gun and fire one (1) to the head this induces a slide lock reload. Then repeat the process.

The drill is shot from the 5 yard line

Ranking
9 seconds NOVICE
8 seconds INTERMEDIATE
7 seconds ADVANCED
6 seconds EXPERT

And one second to each timeline when moving back to the 7 yard line and another second for each at the 10.

El Presidente

This drill is attributed to Jeff Cooper

The drill will work target acquisition, multiple targets and multiple threats (three Targets) and a reload.

The drill was designed to be shot on an IPSC target from 10 yards. I will often use a Sig "Brett" or "Doug" or the US Marshal "Q" or the FLETC ATT-1. Any target with a designated hit zone.

The three (3) Targets will be spaced 1yd from each other shoulder to shoulder

Prep two (2) magazines with three (6) rounds each

Start position: back to targets, hands above shoulders ("surrender position"), pistol concealed

At the start signal, turn, then draw and fire two rounds at each of the three targets. Perform a reload, then fire two rounds at each target again. There should be four hits on each target for a total of twelve.

Ranking
9.0 seconds NOVICE
7.5 seconds INTERMEDIATE
6.0 seconds ADVANCED
5.5 seconds EXPERT

There have been many variations of this drill, including the "Vice-Presidente" which begins with the shooter facing the targets and which is usually performed at 7yd instead of 10yd distance.

The Tactical Presidente

Same set up but this time each target will require 2 to each body and 1 to each head.

Same mag prep so that a reload is required.

The Demi-Presidente

Same target setup as the El Presidente. On signal, turn, draw and fire two shots to each target, reload, then one head shot each.

A good time would be 10 seconds or less.

TRIPLE NICKEL

This drill was designed for the Department of Homeland Security and the US Air Marshals and is shot from the 5 yard line.
The shooter starts from the holstered & concealed position. It was originally designed to be shot on the FLETC Trans Star 2 target. I prefer using the FLETC ATT-1 or the USMS "Q".

Five targets are placed five yards from the shooter with at least 1.5 feet between each target.

Shooter begins with weapon concealed. On the buzzer, shooter must draw and engage each target with two shots.

After the first target is engaged but *before* the last target is engaged, the shooter must perform a reload.

For a shot to count as a hit, it must be completely within the 4/5 scoring zones of a Tran Star-II target or within the bottle of a ATT-1 or USMS "Q" target.

Just like Sig Academy standards hits touching the line or outside the scoring zone are considered a **miss**.

If you have to ask, it is a miss!

The drill was originally developed by David Blinder. The target can be downloaded and printed. The more common version of the target developed by Todd Green. His version of the target has directions conveniently printed under each dot. This version is part of the FLETC ATT-1

> Dot #1- Draw and fire one string of 5 rounds for best group.
> Dot #2- Draw and fire 1 shot, holster and repeat X4,
> Dot #3 and 4- Draw and fire 1 shot on #3, then 1 shot on 4, holster and repeat X4.
> Dot #5- Draw and fire 5 rounds, strong hand only,
> Dot #6 and 7- Draw and fire 2 shots on #6, then 2 on #7, holster, repeat X4.
> Dot #8- From ready fire five shots, support hand only.
> Dot #9 and 10- Draw and fire 1 shots on #9, speed reload, fire 1 shots on #10, holster and repeat X3.

Responsible Citizens Seeking Responsible Training

10-10-10

This drill was designed by Larry Vickers and is designed to test speed and accuracy. 10 rounds fired from 10 yards in 10 seconds.

I was taught to always start from the holster, but depending on your ability, you may start from the ready.

The drill was designed to be shot on a B-8 Bullseye Target, but only into the black of the bullseye. This is a 4 ½ inch circle.

Basic Training CCW Skills Drills   Ken Hackathorn.

3 yards
On the signal draw keeping the gun in the retention position (Gun close to body) and fire 2 rounds center mass. Repeat twice for a total of 6 rounds.

5 yards
On signal draw and fire either 1 round or dedicated pairs firing strong hand only. Fire a total of 6 rounds.

3 yards
On signal back away from the target, draw and fire 3 rounds center mass while moving.

7 yards
On signal draw and fire a dedicated pair center mass, slowly go to ready and scan the area and reholster. Repeat twice for a total of 6 rounds.

7 yards
Move from center of target a few steps. On signal draw and fire 3 rounds center of mass moving laterally across the range. Repeat going in the opposite direction. Move only as fast as you can hit the target.

7 yards
Place firearm on the ground, on the signal with your strong hand tucked into your belt pick up the firearm with your support hand and fire 1 round center of mass. Repeat once for a total of two rounds.

15 yards
Draw and fire 1 round in 2.5 seconds. Repeat twice for a total of 3 rounds. These should be very precise hits. (Hack considers this long range for self-defense, however should be practiced.)

Responsible Citizens Seeking Responsible Training

3-Second Drill　　　　　　　Ken Hackathorn

Range: 5yd Target: three IPSC or IDPA targets spaced at least two feet apart shoulder to shoulder each individual string has a 3-second PAR time.

1. Fire one (and only one) shot at the head of each target, going from left to right

2. Fire one (and only one) shot at the head of each target, going from right to left.

3. Fire one (and only one) shot at the head of each target, beginning with the middle target and then finishing with the two outside targets in any order.

Barrel Drill   Ken Hackathorn

Set up 3 barrels at 10, 15, and 25 yards in a zigzag pattern. Fire 2 rnds at each target from each barrel while kneeling behind cover.

5 yards
From the holster, single headshots for precision

7 yards
From the holster, controlled pairs for precision

7 yards
Out of battery reloads. Begin with one round in the chamber and an empty magazine. Draw and fire one round, reload, fire one round.

7 yards Malfunction clearance drill.
2 dummy rnds & 4 to 6 live rounds per magazine. Draw and fire double taps, TRF for each malfunction.

7 yards Malfunction clearance drill.
Begin at low ready with a failure to eject malfunction created with a piece of empty brass. Come on target, attempt to fire, and clear the stovepipe, fire two rounds.

7 yards Tactical reload drill. Draw and fire two rounds, tactical reload, fire two rounds.

Responsible Citizens Seeking Responsible Training

Gunsite Graduation Drill

This drill, or culmination of drills is a good place to start. The ability to draw and get acceptable hits in an acceptable level of accuracy is a must.

With 1 silhouette target:

1- 3 meters: draw, fire 1 round. Par- 1.5 sec Perform 2x
2- 7 meters: draw, fire 1 round. Par- 1.5 sec Perform 2x
3- 10 meters: draw, fire 1 round. Par- 2.5 sec Perform 2x
4- 15 meters: draw, fire 1 round from kneeling. Par- 3.5 sec Perform 2x
5- 25 meters: draw, fire 2 rounds, from prone. Par- 6.5 sec Perform 1x

10 rounds/50 points possible

I enjoy shooting this on steel. If using steel at distances of less than 10 meters make sure frangible ammo is used.

Circle Drill

George Harris is credited with this drill. George Harris was the lead instructor at the Sig Academy when it started. I have had the pleasure of shooting with and learning from George many times!

Range: 7yd Target: 8" plate Start position: any Rounds fired: 36

The Circle Drill is intended to teach students the relationship between speed and accuracy, and how time affects marksmanship fundamentals.

The drill begins by firing six rounds at the plate at a slow pace (1 shot per second). Repeat. This is fundamental marksmanship with little or no time pressure.

Next, pick up the pace. Fire six rounds at a moderate pace (2 shots per second). Repeat. This speed is the "comfort zone" for most shooters, they should still get reasonably good hits.

Finally, maximize speed by firing six rounds at a pace of about 4 shots per second (or as fast as possible if 4/second is faster than the gun can be kept under control). Repeat.

This pace should push a shooter outside of his comfort zone and force him to work harder at recoil management and sight tracking.

Accuracy will suffer but the goal is to keep 90%+ hits on the plate.

This SHOOTING EVALUATION was the one that I came up with to get away from known times and round counts. The question is simple, can you run a gun and keep it operational.

(The PANDA Skills Assessment) this Course is Black and White

Based on the shooter's Training and Experience, the shooter will be asked to make their own decisions based on their situational awareness. This will be your gun fight, manage it.

Skills Evaluated/Tested : DESCION MAKING; Situational Awareness (Weapon, Target-Facings,/Gone); Magazine preparation, Weapons Loading, Weapons Press Check, Draw, Presentation, Shooting Platform, Trigger Control, Sight Alignment, Sight Picture, Follow Thru and Recovery, Emergency Reloads, Tactical Reloads, Magazine Exchanges, Malfunction Clearing.

Shooter's Briefing (READ VERBATUM TO SHOOTERS)

1. This is an evaluation for intermediate to advanced shooters. Only SAFTEY Decisions will made and controlled by the Range Safety Officer, all engagement decisions will be made by you; this will be your gun fight, manage it.

2. You know how to clear firearm malfunctions. Are there any questions and is a demonstration required to clear any weapon related malfunction? Keep your weapon in an operational condition.

INSTRUCTOR NOTE: Instructor will demonstrate the corrective action required. The student will be allowed to practice the malfunction clearing method

3. You know how and you are proficient in reloading your firearm and keeping it loaded. Are there any questions and is a demonstration required for an emergency reload, magazine exchange, administrative reload, tactical reload with or without retention? Keep your weapon loaded.

INSTRUCTOR NOTE: Instructor will demonstrate the reloading action required. The student will be allowed to practice the reloading method

4. You must keep your firearms in a condition that will allow for fast accurate firing.
5. Alibis will only be granted for falling targets or faulty ammunition
6. You will receive 9 target facings at known distances between1 ½ meters to 10 meters
7. The times of target facings will be unknown
8. You will engage the "threat" with as many accurate shots as you are capable of while the target is presented.
9. You will receive an unknown time between target facings and line distance changes. The shooter must ensure their firearm is prepared for the engagement.

10. THIS IS A TIMED EVENT, THE DISTANCES ARE KNOWN; THE TIMES ARE UNKNOWN; THE AMOUNT OF ROUNDS ACCURATLEY FIRED TO SUCCEED ARE UNKNOWN. YOU DECIDE HOW MANY ROUNDS NEED TO BE FIRED; HOW MANY ACCURATE HITS ARE REQUIRED; HOW MANY MAGAZINZES AND HOW MANY ROUNDS IN EACH MAGAZINE. IT IS YOUR RESPONSIBILITY TO KEEP YOUR FIREARM OPERATING.
11. Off lining is your decision
12. MISSES WILL BE PENALIZED

REQUIREMENTS: One Duty Pistol, Magazines or Speed Loaders (Agency Requirement), One (1) TRANSTAR 4 Target, 100 Rounds of Ammunition for Duty Weapon

PISTOL VERSION (The PANDA Skills Assessment) this Course is Black and White

You will need 100 rounds of ammunition for your weapon

Shooters- load, charge and press check if you wish

STAGE ONE – 1 ½ METER LINE (1) ONE Facing

INSTRUCTOR NOTE: TIME- **2 second facing**

Shooter – one foot on the **1 ½ meter line**. When the target faces, fire as many rounds as you can accurately place in the acceptable area of the target.

INSTRUCTOR NOTE: The commands of "Shooter Ready? Stand By, will be given prior to each facing to ensure SAFETY REQUIREMENTS ARE MET

Shooter- make the line secure, move to the **3 Meter Line**

INSTRUCTOR NOTE: 30 seconds after movement before next target facing

STAGE TWO- 3 METER LINE (2) TWO FACINGS

INSTRUCTOR NOTE: TIME- **3 second facings**

INSTRUCTOR NOTE: The commands of "Shooter Ready? Stand By, will be given prior to each facing to ensure SAFETY REQUIREMENTS ARE MET

1. Shooter – one foot on the **3 meter line**. When the target faces, fire as many rounds as you can accurately place in the acceptable area of the target.

INSTRUCTOR NOTE: 10 Seconds between each facing on the same yard line

2. Shooter – one foot on the 3 meter line. When the target faces, fire as many rounds as you can accurately place in the acceptable area of the target.

Shooter make the line secure, move to the **5 Meter Line**

INSTRUCTOR NOTE: 30 seconds after movement before next target facing

STAGE THREE 5 METER LINE (2) TWO FACINGS

INSTRUCTOR NOTE: TIME- **3 second facings**

Responsible Citizens Seeking Responsible Training

INSTRUCTOR NOTE: The commands of "Shooter Ready? Stand By, will be given prior to each facing to ensure SAFETY REQUIREMENTS ARE MET

1. Shooter – one foot on the **5 meter line**. When the target faces, fire as many rounds as you can accurately place in the acceptable area of the target.

INSTRUCTOR NOTE: 10 Seconds between each facing on the same yard line

2. Shooter – one foot on the **5 meter line**. When the target faces, fire as many rounds as you can accurately place in the acceptable area of the target.

INSTRUCTOR NOTE: 30 seconds after movement before next target facing

STAGE FOUR 7 METER LINE (2) TWO FACINGS

INSTRUCTOR NOTE: TIME- **3 second facings**

INSTRUCTOR NOTE: The commands of "Shooter Ready? Stand By, will be given prior to each facing to ensure SAFETY REQUIREMENTS ARE MET

1. Shooter – one foot on the 7 meter line. When the target faces, fire as many rounds as you can accurately place in the acceptable area of the target.

INSTRUCTOR NOTE: 10 Seconds between each facing on the same yard line

2. Shooter – one foot on the 7 meter line. When the target faces, fire as many rounds as you can accurately place in the acceptable area of the target.

INSTRUCTOR NOTE: 30 seconds after movement before next target facing

STAGE FOUR 10 METER LINE (2) TWO FACINGS

INSTRUCTOR NOTE: TIME- **4 second facings**

INSTRUCTOR NOTE: The commands of "Shooter Ready? Stand By, will be given prior to each facing to ensure SAFETY REQUIREMENTS ARE MET

1. Shooter – one foot on the 10 meter line. When the target faces, fire as many rounds as you can accurately place in the acceptable area of the target.

INSTRUCTOR NOTE: 10 Seconds between each facing on the same yard line

2. Shooter – one foot on the 10 meter line. When the target faces, fire as many rounds as you can accurately place in the acceptable area of the target.

SCORING: Any hits on the FLETC ATT-1 Target or the USMS Target

Any hits in the 5 ring of the Transtar 4 target are counted as One (1) Point (50 Points to meet the standard)

Any hits in the 3 or 1 zone of the Transtar 4 target are not counted as scoreable hits. These hits do no hurt you, they do not help you.

Any Hits located in the White area are a DNQ- Option, score DNQ hits as a MINUS 2 ½ points

Ultimate PANDA Standard

Target ATT-1
Shots in the 8 inch circle count as 1 point
Shots in the Orange body are neutral
Shots in the white...**DNQ**

"There is a tremendous difference between Shooting Methods that work well when you are simply trying to put holes in the target and those that work well when the target is trying to put holes in you"
Col Rex Applegate

Always strive to maintain a high degree of accuracy in your training sessions. It will serve you well in case you ever have to use your weapon for real. Speed is fine…..
Accuracy is final.

Finial Thoughts:

It's not the will to win that matters- everyone has that. It's the will to prepare to win that matters.

Bear Bryant

Responsible Citizens Seeking Responsible Training

**"Train hard like your life depends on it
Train safe like your life depends on it,
I hope to see you on the range!"
Kyle**

http://www.modernamericancombativearts.com/

www.**modernamericancombativearts**.com/youtube.htm

www.facebook.com/modcombat/?nr

https://www.instagram.com/**modernamericancombativearts**

"There is a tremendous difference between Shooting Methods that work well when you are simply trying to put holes in the target and those that work well when the target is trying to put holes in you"
Col Rex Applegate

Always strive to maintain a high degree of accuracy in your training sessions. It will serve you well in case you ever have to use your weapon for real. Speed is fine…..
Accuracy is final.

Finial Thoughts:

It's not the will to win that matters- everyone has that. It's the will to prepare to win that matters.

Bear Bryant

Responsible Citizens Seeking Responsible Training

> "Train hard like your life depends on it
> Train safe like your life depends on it,
> I hope to see you on the range!"
> Kyle

http://www.modernamericancombativearts.com/

www.**modernamericancombativearts**.com/youtube.htm

www.facebook.com/modcombat/?nr

https://www.instagram.com/**modernamericancombativearts**

Responsible Citizens Seeking Responsible Training

www.ingramcontent.com/pod-product-compliance
Lightning Source LLC
Chambersburg PA
CBHW070620160426
43194CB00009B/1325